The Essential Guide
for Study Abroad
in the United Kingdom

Holly R. Carter

University Press of America,® Inc.

Copyright © 2004 by
University Press of America,® Inc.
4501 Forbes Boulevard
Suite 200
Lanham, Maryland 20706
UPA Acquisitions Department (301) 459-3366

PO Box 317
Oxford
OX2 9RU, UK

All rights reserved
Printed in the United States of America
British Library Cataloging in Publication Information Available

Library of Congress Control Number: 2003117174
ISBN 0-7618-2846-X (paperback : alk. ppr.)

∞™ The paper used in this publication meets the minimum
requirements of American National Standard for Information
Sciences—Permanence of Paper for Printed Library Materials,
ANSI Z39.48—1984

Dedications

Many thanks to all of those who made this book possible. To the International Centre of University of Surrey Roehampton for all of their input and patience, to ASA 2001 and RIS 2001-2002, with the help of Nick Anglewicz, Simon Davey, and David Powell. To Life Sciences at University of Surrey Roehampton for their help and friendship. To Kenneth Quin for being part of the family.

To Dr. David Martin for starting me on my way to my first adventure. To Campbell and Irene Shaw for being my family while in Glasgow. To the Rotary Clubs of Wichita Falls and Greenock and Gourock Scotland for giving me the opportunity to study abroad.

To my family for letting me follow my dreams, wherever in the world they take me. To Mark for helping with this project and always listening.

Contents

Foreword ix
Preface xiii
Acknowledgment xvii
Chapter 1 Introduction 1
Chapter 2 Leaving Home 5
    Shipping 13
    Visas 13
    Overseas Air Travel 14
    Information/ Paperwork Check List 16
    Packing Guide 17
Chapter 3 Arriving in the UK 19
    Useful Tips for the First Weeks 19
    Immigration at the Airport: 19
    Arriving at Your University: 21
    Jet Lag 22
    Other Possibilities for the First Weeks 24
    Budget 25
    Jobs 27
    An Emotional Time 28
Chapter 4 Academics 31
    Titles 33
    Classes 33
    Assessment 34
    Essays 34
    Exams 37
    Grades 38
    Time Tables, Schedules, and Calendars 39
    Academic Pitfalls 39
Chapter 5 Living in the UK 41
    Useful Places 41
    The Post Office 41
    The Bank 42
    The Doctor/ National Health Service 43
    Eating in the UK 44
    Restaurants, Pubs, Typical Food, Cost of Food 44
    Grocery Shopping 46
    A Taste of Home 46
    Useful Tips 47
Special Section: Dr. H's Top UK Tips 55

Chapter 6 Travel in the UK 59
    Essential Travel.. 59
    Sightseeing in the UK 62
Chapter 7 Travel in Europe 71
    Airfare 71
    Ferries 72
    Hostels 74
    Eurostar 74
  Places to Go... 75
    France- Paris 75
    Belgium - Brussels, Bruges 76
    Netherlands - Amsterdam 77
    Spain - Madrid and Ibiza 77
    Italy - Rome, Pisa, Venice 77
    Ireland - Dublin 78
  Travel Cost Work Sheet 79
Chapter 8 Advice From the Experts 85
  What do you wish that you had been told before leaving to study abroad? 85
  What has been the most frustrating thing about studying abroad? 87
  What is the best thing about studying abroad? 89
  What have you learned by studying abroad? 91
  If you could give a student who is about to leave to study in the UK advice before they leave, what would you tell them? 93
Chapter 9 Getting Ready to Return Home 97
    Packing your Bags 97
    Posting Items Home 99
    Getting to the Airport 99
    Other Suggestions 100
    It Is Difficult to Leave 101
Chapter 10 Home Again 103
    Ideas for Sharing Your Experience with Others 105
Chapter 11 My Trip 111
    Pre Departure: 112
    First Week 114
    Budget 116
    Academics 118
    Living in the UK 120
Appendix A: My Journal 125
Appendix B: Useful Web Addresses 129
    Airline Websites 129
    Other Travel Sites 129
    Groceries in the UK 130
    Travel in the UK Websites 130
    Places to Visit 130
    City and Places of Interest Website 130

Travel outside of the UK Websites 132
Author.. 135
Index 137

Foreword

The impact of globalisation and mass communication is such that the world appears to be shrinking. There is increasing economic cooperation between nations although in many cases cultural differences are still significant and even appear to be growing. In these circumstances people who have had experience of living and working in more than one country have an inherent advantage over their peers. They learn that there is more than one world view; they learn to adapt quickly in order to operate effectively in another culture; they learn about superficial similarities and deep seated differences and vice versa; they learn to hold on to what they hold dear about their homeland but to let go of their prejudices. In our rapidly changing world we need people like this. You have taken the first step to becoming one of these rare and valuable individuals by choosing to extend your intellectual horizons and to study abroad.

All universities are enriched by the presence of international students who bring another dimension to the learning and teaching environment. You will find that you are a novelty and that your opinion is sought on many matters. You will be regarded as a representative and a spokesperson for your country and will have the opportunity to hear other differing but equally valid viewpoints on a wide range of issues. Many universities in the United Kingdom have a student body drawn from more than a hundred different countries and this will provide you with a myriad of opportunities and will promote within you an enhanced international awareness. You will get the most from this environment if you actively engage with students from many different cultures rather than staying within your own comfort zone. After all you have chosen to embark on this new and exciting experience.

The time that you will be away from your home country almost certainly will be the most stimulating and challenging period of your life so far. You will want to embrace every part of it, especially if it is for a very limited period, such as a semester. Your energy should go into making friends, achieving your study objectives, travelling within the UK and Europe, and having as many new experiences as possible. In this way you will grow inestimably as a person and will return home with new skills, knowledge and understanding, and new friends to visit across the globe.

Making the decision to study abroad in the United Kingdom for a semester, a year or longer is probably one of the biggest decisions that you have ever taken. You will have spent much time choosing the right country, the right location, the right university, and the right courses. However, all this is just the start of the decision making process. You will now have to consider accommodation, finances, immigration, travel and even more prosaic matters such as luggage allowances.

Over the past six years I have been privileged to meet many students who come to the UK to study, to live and to make friends for life. They are often in contact with my staff in the International Centre at the University of Surrey Roehampton for many months before they arrive in the UK. They have questions about their programme, the campus, what the weather will be like in London, what they should bring and on one occasion we even had a student who wanted to know the colour of the décor of her bedroom so that she could coordinate her accessories accordingly! Even though Roehampton, like most universities, provides its own specific literature for students coming to study from overseas it would have been helpful to be able to alleviate some of their natural anxieties by referring them to a book such as this, written by someone who has been through the experience both as a student coming from the USA to study in the UK and then a number of years later as a member of staff at Roehampton who chose to volunteer to help international students find their feet and so pass on some of the practical wisdom that she has accumulated.

Study abroad advisers in your home university are also often on the receiving end of numerous queries from students who are preparing to leave their university to embark on a study period overseas. They too will find this book extremely useful. It is not designed to replace the care and attention that students need when preparing for travel, but to assist them in becoming more self-reliant and to have the confidence to make thorough preparations knowing that they are covering all the bases.

In addition to practical information (and I have learned never to underestimate the level of detail about practical matters that some students need) this book addresses important issues such a culture shock and the structure of academic life in the UK. These can be 'make or break' areas for some students. Very few students return home because they forgot to pack a winter coat, but a number do leave, sometimes after a very short period of time, because they have not prepared themselves for the university environment in the UK. Universities here require a much more self directed, independent style of learning than in many other countries. Classes are not generally compulsory but students are expected to do significant amounts of studying in their own time and the mark for a course may all depend on a single piece of work or one examination. It is important for study abroad students to understand the implications of this and to adapt their learning style relatively speedily. Most will do so and they will have a fulfilling experience.

The social culture may also be more alien than anticipated. It is often said that the USA and the UK are two totally different cultures joined by a single language and there is some truth in this. Getting involved with student life is important and this is often best done through the Students' Union and its associated clubs and societies. Students arriving in September will be at an advantage as they will be new at university at the same time as thousands of UK students. Students arriving at other times of the year will have to work harder at developing a social network and engaging with activities run by the Students' Union and the International Office will help in this.

You will, of course want to make time to travel and explore while studying in the UK. This book is an excellent starting point for information about places to visit for days out, for the weekend and for longer trips. It also provides practical tips on different modes of travel and, finally, useful advice on your journey home and how you can best share your experience of studying abroad with others.

This book is an indispensable tool to assist you during the period before you depart for the UK, while you are away and when you return home after what will be a life changing experience. You will be dealing with new situations on a daily, initially perhaps even hourly, basis and the reassurance that this book provides may prove to be a lifesaver on more than one occasion. It will also provide some reassurance and peace of mind to your parents and family back home.

Use this book to prepare yourself, to reassure yourself and to learn about new possibilities. Read what the experts say; they have been through the experience and thrived on it. It is a privilege to have the opportunity to immerse yourself in another culture and you will find that you will return home more independent, more questioning, someone who dares to challenge the status quo and who looks for new and enriching experiences. Your own personal growth will enable you to take your place in our increasingly diverse world with confidence and the knowledge, skills and understanding that you have accumulated while studying in the UK will be yours for life. Go for it; you will never regret having done so.

Dr. Heather Forland
Director
International Centre
University of Surrey Roehampton
London

Preface

This book is the culmination of long term, participant observation research abroad, or perhaps it is easier to say that the book is partly my story and partly the story of the many people that I have been fortunate enough to work with. The project actually started many years ago, in 1996 I believe, but the journey has taken me until 2002 to write this text. In the time that elapsed I have learned from myself and learned from others, but I always believed that this book needed to be written. I hope that you have confirmed this as you are reading it now, and you are the audience that it has always been intended for, a curious, clever student who has a desire to travel and make their way in the world.

I came to study abroad by complete accident. One day in my undergraduate institution I saw a flyer on a bulletin board for a study abroad scholarship. I knew that I liked to travel and I also knew that I was a penniless student working my way through university, sometimes with as many as four jobs at a time and a full time course load. I picked up the flyer and was off to find Dr. David Martin, a wonderful man who told me more about the scholarship. I applied but it was three long years until I actually received the scholarship. During the many incarnations of my application, I changed and changed the proposal. Having always wanted to study in France, this was my first choice. Finding my language skills diminishing over the three years, I turned to the UK.

By this time I was already enrolled in a doctoral program and my focus was health care and to some extent, the health care system of the UK. So it was only natural that I apply for a UK location. I chose University of Glasgow because of a visiting lecturer at my home university from Scotland who seemed nice enough. I had no idea what a wonderful choice this would be. Only now do I see how brilliant this selection was.

I had no book like this to prepare for my journey, and knew no one who had been abroad to study or live. I was able to visit with a student who had been the year before. We had lunch together and talked over some of the details. This was very informative, and the only real help that I was given. I had a tour book, but it didn't give the type of information that one needs for this type of a stay. So, I left for my journey like every student I have seen since: over packed and no idea of what was ahead.

My time at Glasgow was amazing. I completed a master's degree, made wonderful friends, learned about a new culture, enjoyed sightseeing, and grew as a person. I always wondered if this journey was unique or was just the same thing that many people found. I had no way to know, and no one told me anything about how the time abroad would change me, how to deal with returning home, how friends and family would react, and how to cope with all of the changes.

I came back to the United States with the intention of finishing my doctorate and returning overseas to do more work. By this time my research interest was firmly in the health care system of the United Kingdom, a difficult area to research from the US. Everyday as I worked diligently on my dissertation I would take a break and look attentively for jobs in the UK. I guess I never really expected to get a job since it is so difficult to get a visa to live in the UK, and I really had little experience, which is key to getting entrance clearance.

When I came to work on my dissertation one day, I received an e-mail telling me that I had been short listed for a job at a university in London. I did not even know what short listed meant. I actually had to go to the international center of my university and ask. There an e-mail was sent around the world to get comments about short listing. When I got a serious response, I bought a plane ticket.

I was in the UK within a week or two of the e-mail and had a job within a day or two of my arrival. I had just six weeks to pack up my life, finish my dissertation, and move to another country. But I was eager and made my way through all of these tasks, in order to move sometime in August 1999.

I started working at the university that same month, and the one thing that shocked me was how little I knew about universities in the UK, even though I had a degree from one. All of those funny things that they spoke about really meant nothing to me. I had no idea what invigilating, a 2:1 or A4 paper were. I would simply go to the course convener and make sure I was in good standing. If she said yes, then I was happy. So here I was lost, in a mass of new words and new culture. I had to learn what a second marker, external examiner, and an exam board were. When asked to invigilate I told the secretary that I was happy to do it, I just needed to know what it was.

In the middle of all of the differences in my work world, I also had masses of confusion about life. How do I buy groceries? How do I get my bank account? How do I ride the tube, train, and bus? I spent many days lost and a lot of time asking directions. I can remember riding train after train trying to get home and being so relieved once I was there.

Perhaps this was all confounded by the fact that I was doing it alone while making money to support myself, feed myself, and entertain myself. I never realized how my life was filled with other people. I had never had to eat alone or buy a movie ticket for one. Eventually, I grew skilled at which restaurants were best for a party of one, what times were best to eat, to shop or to go to the cinema. I even volunteered locally at the Putney Arts Theatre, a wonderful place where I made friends that will last forever.

I did all of these things alone for a semester before I realized that there were other students who were going through the same culture shock but were not united to help each other. This became my mission. So over the next weeks the word went out and we had a meeting. We eventually became the American Student Association (ASA). The wonderful people that I met there are still my friends to this day. Caroline, Laurel, Mary Kate, Jeff, Cheryl, Brian, Nat, David, Christy, Nick, Peter, Simon, Pedro, Akiko, Mitsumi, and all of the others who made my life such fun. As a group we went on trips - some near and some far - shared meals, had parties, shared our ups and downs, but most importantly we shared our information.

In the next semester the group grew, some trips had almost 200 students on them. This is all due to the fact that we only worked as a collective. Able to share our frustrations and joys, able to find others who were going through the same things, others who had the same fears and emotions, we were a large cohesive group. Working with all of the students made me realize that my experience in Scotland was not that different from the experience these student were having.

Through these students and my own experience, I am able to write this book. There is a commonality in all who study abroad. There are questions about the culture and the people, there are curiosities that you will always remember, but there is also an emotion and growth that people share. I want this book to be the reassurance that you are on the right path and a map of how the path works. You will have your own experiences and, perhaps, find things that are not included in this book. But this gives you a guide to your time abroad.

Study abroad is about so much more than university and academics. Many find that classes take a backseat to their adventures and the tremendous personal growth that they experience. You may find that study abroad is about growing up, travel, independence, self sufficiency, making new friends, or finding out what you really didn't like about your life at home. It is not an escape or a permanent solution for problems and can be difficult at times. But take the challenge and face the difficult times ahead. It is living through them that will give you growth and strength.

Many years after leaving Scotland, I was asked to return to speak to a group there about my time abroad. When thinking back on my student experience, it was so powerful in my life that I had to wait many years to talk about it. I told them about how I grew as a person and found out what the true kindness of others was. I also told them that for the first time that I ever remember, I was forced to go further. I guess I found it easier to express as a metaphor, so I told them that when I went to Loch Ness I stood outside the entire time looking for the monster Nessie, even though it was cold and raining. When the music played I danced the Dashing White Sergeant. Even though I didn't know the steps, I still danced.

I hope you take this time abroad to dance, and realize that you cannot limit yourself only to what you know how to do. You too can dance the Dancing White Sergeant if you want to badly enough.

Have a wonderful time and make the most of this special opportunity.

Acknowledgment

In writing this book I would like to acknowledge my friends and co-workers who helped me put this all together, my publisher for giving me the opportunity to get this message out, and all of those who helped me learn this information in my time abroad. Many people took the time to explain differences, meanings, and culture. This book would not be possible without all of them. I am also grateful to Mary Hjelm for her time and help.

Chapter 1
Introduction

As you are looking at this book, or hopefully taking it out to start your journey abroad, I can only say congratulations for getting this far! I tell all students that getting your location and program details worked out are a majority of the battle. Now it is time to have fun, study, and learn a lot about another culture, academics, and mostly about yourself. This book is designed to help you do that by giving you a crash course through some of the information that you will need to know and some of the more peculiar parts of life in the United Kingdom.

This book is an introduction and a guide to many things about study abroad in the United Kingdom. It is also a book that is not about many things. It is not designed to show you how to enroll in programs abroad, how to find programs, scholarships, or to make recommendations about programs and universities. This book is written for students who have already organized their study abroad courses and are looking for a guide that gives more information than a traditional travel guide. I do recommend that you take a travel book along with you to your destination, as it will have valuable information for sightseeing, restaurants, and practical tips. But, this book serves to pick up where the travel guide leaves off with different information that someone staying for longer than a vacation will need.

Most students will have started this journey through international offices, web searches, and by gathering materials. You may have spent months applying for programs, have finally been accepted, and know that you are going. Now is the time that this book is designed to come in handy. The book covers pre-departure, living abroad, academics, travel, and returning home. The book should be a resource for your entire trip, before it begins and after it ends.

The book does speak in generalities at times, as all universities are different. But I am sure that you know universities in your home country can differ from place to place, and the UK is no exception. You will need to gather information specific to your circumstances on your own, but the book gives ideas about what you should know, the usual places to find information, and how universities work in general.

Using this guide may also help you to see what other students have experienced and what they have felt and thought throughout the process. Many find studying abroad a time of tremendous growth and development, but remember that sometimes these are difficult things to do. The thoughts of others may reassure you that you are following a path known to others, and that you are not alone.

The book is divided into twelve chapters that address the time you will spend preparing for your experience, the first weeks, living and studying abroad, and your journey home. You may want to read the book thoroughly before you go and use it as a guide when you are abroad. Many things may not be entirely clear until you see them for yourself, and then you can use the book as a reference. The book also includes a chapter to customize your questions and experiences, and a log that you can take home as a memory of your time abroad.

As when writing about any country - in this case about four different countries - it is important to note that although there are many similarities between places there are also many differences. If you live in a large city rather than a small village, there will be differences. If you live in Scotland rather than England or in the north rather than the south of the country, you may find things very diverse. There is no one common trait between people. You will have to adjust to your particular circumstances both geographically and socially. The different countries in the UK can seem like different worlds; but, the experience is about learning and taking advantage of whatever is available to you.

Don't be surprised if you find yourself lost at first. Everyone gets lost, but remember to ask questions. This was one of the most difficult things for me when I first moved abroad. I didn't want to look as if there were things I did not know. I got over this shyness very quickly and probably asked too many questions. Besides being confused, you will probably be lonely and homesick too. Take these as opportunities to grow, meet new people, and appreciate what you have. Many times we are not pushed to go outside of our comfortable social circle, to meet new people, or even to appreciate all of those who are supporting us in this time abroad. The difficult times will be a learning experience themselves if you use them productively rather than wasting time being upset. If you miss friends and family, send them a letter or a small gift. If you are lonely, go out and make new friends. My rule of thumb when I moved to a new place abroad was to never turn down an invitation.

Take this opportunity to learn as much as possible. You will learn in your classes and you will learn about another culture, but mostly you will learn about yourself. This self awareness of your inner strength, your ability to handle the difficult times, and perhaps a better awareness of what is important to you, will be something that will last a lifetime. Whenever I think I can not do something, I often reflect on all of the things that I have done, by myself, in strange and foreign places and I am confident in my ability to handle new challenges.

I hope this guide is useful and the information makes the trip less stressful and the environment easier to understand. While I can give you these tips and this information, only you can make the trip unique and unforgettable. I hope that you, like many of my own students, will be able to say that you had the time of your life.

Chapter 2
Leaving Home

You have probably been through months of forms, applications, and planning. Now you have been accepted to a program in the United Kingdom and the real planning begins. This is the time to look at specific ideas about what to bring, how to pack it, and what to do if you have too much. This is the more practical side of actually leaving your home country on your trip abroad. Planning can make all of the difference in your experience. I have known students who planned too little and found that their scarce funds went to buying more expensively priced items that they could have brought from home. I have also seen people who planned too much, and I can assure you that your luggage allowance will not let you bring a different outfit for every possible occasion.

Try to strike a balance between too little and too much planning. If done correctly, you will not have to worry when you arrive at your new university, and you will have less stress before you leave. A packing list and a check list are included at the end of the chapter. I would advise you to make a copy of this and use it as a guide. Personalize it and make adjustments based on all of the information that you get from others and from your new university.

I always advise students to try and speak to someone who has been abroad and, hopefully, to your university before leaving. Sometimes you can get names and contact details through your home university's international office, or the university abroad may give you some details. One of the best sources about any place is the students who have been previously. Glossy brochures aside, this is the best way to be prepared. I would suggest arranging to speak to or meet a student who has been abroad in the three months before you leave. If you can make an appointment to discuss a list of questions, then you have time to ask all of the things that you forgot to ask the first time! Most students love to talk about their time abroad so it is usually a positive experience for both parties.

You do need those glossy brochures though. They will have vital information for you about location and features of your university. I would advise you to read them from cover to cover at home then tear out the pages that you want to take with you. No need to take the whole thing and waste luggage allowance. Some of the vital information generally contained in the prospectus is both course material and university information. You may have also received a package or letters from your UK university's international office that ranges from orientation times and places to your accommodation's location. You will need some of this information for immigration, something we will discuss later in the chapter, but mostly is the useful information that you need to take with you or leave for your friends and family.

<u>Pre Departure Information</u>

As mentioned earlier, the information you receive from your university is valuable to you personally and to immigration. The best way to stay organized is to keep a folder of everything you receive. Before you travel, you will need to go through this to find the most important information to take. The information will be divided into three types: practical information, course information, and immigration information. All other material is at your discretion. I would advise you to leave it at home to make a scrapbook later. Paper can be one of the heaviest things to take with you.

Practical information is the letters and information that you have received about your accommodations, meal plans, off campus housing, orientation sessions, registration dates, international student activities, and other events. You may have received these from several different offices of the university. Some universities offer on campus accommodations, while others will have temporary places to stay while you find off campus housing. Either way have the details of the place and its actual physical address. If you arrive and have to find it yourself this is invaluable. You will also want to leave this information with friends and family. If you have to find accommodation ask the university to put you in contact with the office that lists flats in the area. Almost every university will have this facility. Most offer a list of places close to campus for rent to students. You can use this list to make phone calls, determine an appropriate rental amount, and to make appointments to look at accommodations. Always keep in mind that your university may have extra rooms after the initial move in is complete. Some students will not arrive and others may leave, so you can check on campus accommodations after the first week.

Orientation may be the first time that you meet other international students. Use this time to get questions answered or problems sorted out. Do not miss this session. Although you could think that you have been oriented to university life, there are things about any new university that you need to know. It will also put you into contact with student groups, travel options, and perhaps to meet friends or others who are in the same position as you. I have been told by many students that orientation is one of the most valuable classes that they ever attended. Make plans to arrive the day before orientation, or even a few days before, rather than trying to arrive when classes start. The time before classes may set the tone for your whole experience abroad.

If you are going for a short term study abroad, a summer or a semester program, information may be quite straight forward about the course or courses you are taking. Have this with you so that you know who your contact person is in the UK. Look for valuable schedules that will help you plan your free time. If you are going for a year or longer, then the academic contact details are the most important information. Although your international officer may be able to help, some questions can only be answered by an academic.

If you are attending a semester abroad program, you may have already selected courses approved by your home institution. Have this list with you. If the UK university has not enrolled you in these classes, or if the classes fill before you arrive, then you may have to retrace your steps. If you can get confirmation ahead of time that you have been enrolled it may save you time and a lot of phone calls. If you do arrive and find that courses have been filled, then go directly to the professor and ask for special permission to enroll. Overseas students are sometimes given priority.

Even if you have no problems enrolling in the courses, it is valuable to know who is teaching them and to say hello before the classes start. In either case, having the list of courses that you need to enroll in or have been enrolled in is a must. Keep contact details of professors at hand, and a general overview of the program is good to have as well. If you are going to do an entire degree, these details may help you get into the right classes. The best way to keep on track with this is to do it yourself. You may have spoken to an advisor at home or abroad, but ultimately you are responsible for your own courses and success.

We will talk about immigration at length later in the chapter, but you will need your entry clearance form ahead of time. You need to seek advice from the British Consulate in your home country and start working on this paperwork months before you leave. You will need your letter of acceptance to the university on letterhead paper, copies of your bank statement and a return ticket home. If you an American citizen and are in the country for less than six months, you can enter on a tourist visa alone and do not need this information for entry clearance, but have it for entry to the country. Otherwise you need all of this in its original, the phone number of who to contact in case there is a problem, copies of all documents in case you need them, and you need to have it all out and ready to be presented at passport control. We will go through this in detail later, but if you do not have this paperwork before you leave then you will need to ask the university to send it. This is the most important item that you can pack. Without it you may be sent home before you ever reach the university. If you are not a US citizen, you must check with the British Consulate before leaving the US. It is advisable to do this many months ahead of time and receive directions on getting a visa to enter the UK as a student.

What to Bring

When students ask about packing for a trip, I offer some general advice, most of which is contained in this section. Everyone is different, though, when it comes to taking their own things. My advice is to pack on the light side and supplement when you arrive. Universities in the UK are casual, with some opportunities for more formal dress. The most important factor in knowing what you want to bring is to think about what you can not live without. Pack this and then consider what else you need.

I generally suggest that you pack your suitcases about a week ahead of time and make sure that they are within the weight and size allowance for your flights. Then, over that week, take out about one forth to one half of what you have packed. Unlike vacations or other time you may have spent abroad, you will have access to laundry facilities and the time to shop if you forget something. Most people bring too much and then have trouble getting it all back home. Try to avoid this.

In terms of things to bring, we will divide them into four categories: household/dorm room items, clothing and outerwear, practical items for the climate, and miscellaneous items.

Household/ Dorm Room Items

If you are staying in university accommodations one of the most important questions to ask is about what is supplied and what you need. Most rooms come with a bed and some bed linen, such as a pillow, sheet set, and duvet. Most do not come with towels and you will need to bring these with you. I always suggest bringing towels and other items that you can leave rather than bringing them back with you. So find a good sale before you go. Most flats come with some cooking items, such as pots and pans. If you discover that you need more when you get there, then it is best to buy them abroad. These are heavy items to carry and you may be able to share the expense with other flat mates.

Do not carry too many toiletry items such as toothpaste and shampoo. You will need some to get started with but will have to buy them in your new country in any case. I would suggest bringing a small, inexpensive container of shampoo and conditioner, toothpaste, and other personal hygiene items with you; then, shop for them in bigger sizes over the first week. Again, these are items which will be heavy to carry home and can be left behind for more room in your luggage when you return.

US electronic devices will not work in the UK without a converter or adaptor, as the UK runs on 220 volts and the US on 110. The plugs are also three pronged and shaped differently from the US system. If you attempt to plug any US devices into UK plugs without the proper converters or adapters, your appliances and electronics will be ruined. In most cases it is better to invest in an inexpensive appliance abroad, like a small CD player or radio, a hair dryer, or other hair accessories. If you must take any of this from home, especially a hair dryer, then make sure to get an adaptor powerful enough for the particular device. You can buy these at most retail stores.

Laptop computers generally have automatic adaptors to change to 220 volts to work in Europe (check the power adaptor to make sure it has 110V – 220V written on it). Most universities will have computer labs and printers available for you. Check to see the hours and equipment before you leave. If you need your own laptop or want to have it, some accommodations that have been built recently have internet access. I would suggest that you carefully consider taking any other appliances. They are generally heavy, can take a lot of room and are expensive to buy the converters and transformers for. It is generally easier to get inexpensive items in your study country that you know will work, and leave them for students to come or sell them for a little of the money back.

Clothing and Outerwear

As mentioned previously most universities are very casual. You will need several good pairs of trousers and jeans. I would also pack at least one pair of shorts, as you may need these either to travel to warmer climates or when the weather is nice. Pack a wardrobe that is easily changeable. With this in mind, pack both long and short sleeved t-shirts and sweaters and sweat shirts that you can layer. This way you are prepared for both colder and warmer temperatures.

Remember that washing facilities at universities may not be the most modern, and leaving clothes to wash and dry always creates a risk of them being stolen. I would not take any item that you would be devastated to lose. (I have lost many name brand blue jeans in the laundries of universities in the UK.) I had several pairs and always replaced them with something less expensive. Plus the wear and tear of your time abroad will take its toll. Bring enough of all of your items so that you can go for some time without washing. If you travel you will need at least seven days worth of outfits. Plan so that you are not always running out of any item as there are many better places to spend your evenings than in the laundry.

Perhaps the most important item for you to bring is a good pair or two of comfortable shoes. A pair of tennis shoes is a must and another pair or two of walking shoes. You may love to wear high heels, but you will not love them if you have to walk a mile to the grocery store. Pack for the lifestyle that you will lead; active with a lot of walking. If you are in a big city then you will be on buses, subways, and trains. A comfortable wardrobe and a few pairs of shoes will be your best investment.

Most universities also provide a lively nightlife, and most students make it to the nightlife off campus as well. Generally students will bring items that are more appropriate for clubs. I am always amazed at what one can wear in the cold (especially girls!). I have been out in sweaters and a coat and seen people in the equivalent of a swimsuit. The only advice I can give on this is to bring a couple of outfits that you would be comfortable to go out in and enjoy the nightlife. Not everyone dresses up for this, but you will most likely want to at some point.

Dinners are often given for international students as well as more formal evenings arranged by the university. You will want to take one nice outfit with you that can be used for these occasions. For guys a tie and jacket will be fine. If it is formal enough for a tuxedo, you will want to rent one. For ladies a nice dress that can be dressed up or down is important. If you are on a scholarship that requires you to attend more formal events, then you will need to adjust your wardrobe for this. Almost every semester that one studies abroad, there will be something more formal; so be prepared.

You will need a heavy jacket if you are going abroad in the winter months. I would not suggest anything as warm as a down jacket, but a winter coat, gloves, hat, and scarf are a must. If you going in the spring, a light jacket may be needed almost every day. For both light or heavy jackets, look for ones that are waterproof or that wash up easily. If you are wearing them to pubs and clubs where mysterious beverages can be spilled on them, this will be important.

Always have an umbrella with you, even when it is sunny. If you can buy the smallest umbrella that you can find it should fit easily into any bag. I suggest you purchase a small backpack or larger carry bag to take with you at all times. This will allow you to carry a jacket, umbrella, camera, and other items. Make sure this bag has a zipper. It is much safer.

Practical Items

Any medications that you regularly take will need to be packed in your carry on luggage. If these are prescriptions make sure to get enough to last for your time abroad. Your physician's prescription will not be valid in the UK. To get a prescription filled you will need to see a doctor. If you can bring enough with you for your time abroad, this will be the best option. Any non prescription medicine that you take or need to have in case you are ill should be packed as well. Although you can get some of the same items in UK, people generally like what they know works. So pack a travel collection of items you may need. I always make an assortment for just about any problem. This means that I carry an extra little bag with everything from headache to upset stomach medicine.

A battery powered alarm clock is one of the most practical items one can pack. You can take it to travel anywhere and it is not a problem with the electricity. Some people like to take a travel pouch made especially to take on vacations or neck pouch to keep passports and money in while they are out. These are a matter of preference. Some people feel safer with them.

Bring photographs of your friends, family and home. Make a small album of photos to have with you and to show your friends. This will not only help to make your new place more like home, but will help with conversation or when you are homesick. Bring any other items that may make the time abroad more comfortable, such as your favorite teddy bear or lucky baseball cap. They may make some days better for you. New places can be scary, so a touch of home will help.

Miscellaneous Items

I would strongly urge you not to bring books and not to bring school supplies, which you can buy in the shops or on campus. Unless you are working with one text that is so valuable that you must have it, books are heavy and take up a lot of space. CDs and music that you like are much better to bring and will keep you entertained.

Packing

I have suggested packing a week before you go so you will see the items that you need as well as some of the items that you can live without. There are two other variables that need to be considered when traveling. The first is luggage allowance. Typically airlines will allow you two 70 pound bags to check in and one carry on and one personal item, such as a purse, briefcase, or laptop. Every airline differs, so call ahead and make sure what your particular airline allows. Follow this strictly, otherwise you may be forced to repack at the airport or pay to take things with you.

If you pack wisely, you will pack one suitcase of things that will return and another with things that can be left behind. This will ensure that you have room to pack all of the souvenirs, course items, and gifts that you wish to take home. If you don't plan ahead you may have the limit when you leave, but be over the limit when you return. This is where the items that I have suggested buying abroad will be most helpful.

The other factor to consider is carrying these suitcases. Most universities do not have elevators and are not required to. Most flats and accommodation do not have elevators either. You will be responsible for your luggage through customs, through the airport, perhaps on public transportation, and into your new accommodations. In addition you may need to stay in short term accommodations and then move again. Try to be reasonable; whatever you take is your responsibility to carry. If you must take several large suitcases, be prepared to pay for a taxi rather than public transport. You may find this a trade between taking a smaller amount and using the extra money to buy new things, or taking more and spending the money on cab fare.

Shipping

In the worst case scenario, or if you are going abroad for a longer degree program, you may want to ship some items. Some of the best items to ship are books or paper items because these go at special reduced rates. You can take advantage of these lower prices and pack other items in your luggage that would cost more to ship. If you need to ship items, try and do so ahead of time so you can take advantage of the surface shipping rates. This may mean that your packages do not arrive for many months; but, if you can ship early they can be there when you arrive or shortly after. You will need to prepare for this contingency, as it must be done two to three months before you leave. If you must ship some goods via air mail, try and make good decisions. Air mail is very expensive. Go early to the post office for the rates rather than taking everything there, because you may change your mind when you see the shipping fees.

If you are planning to move abroad for some time and wish to take furniture or other items, contact an international mover for the best rates. These items can take a long time to arrive as they must be searched in customs and you may be charged VAT (value added tax) on them.

Visas

If you are a US citizen, you will need a student visa if you plan to stay in the country more than six months. So unless you are going on a very short exchange, you will need one. You will also need an entry clearance, which you must apply for from the British Consulate. Then your visa will be issued in the airport at Passport Control when you arrive in the country. Contact the UK consulate in the United States before leaving to make sure that these rules have not changed. With the ever changing status of immigration regulations, it best to prepare ahead of time.

When being issued a visa upon arrival, the Passport Control agent will look over your documentation, as mentioned above, and stamp a visa in your passport for the length of your stay. You must leave once this visa has expired, or extend the visa at the Home Office in the UK. Staying past the length of your visa is a violation of UK law and you can be sent home. Most letters of acceptance from your UK university will give the length of the course, and visas will be issued for an appropriate time length to complete your studies. Any other issues should be discussed with your international officer or the UK Consulate before leaving. Be aware that extending your visa through the Home Office can sometimes take a long time to do. You may also have to send your passport away to do so. Be prepared and work on this early.

Overseas Air Travel

When packing your carry-on luggage, remember to include your papers for Passport Control, contact information for your university, and any other information about your pick up, transfer, or directions. You will also want to change some money before arrival in case you need to make an emergency phone call, buy food and drinks, or take a taxi.

Regardless of where you are flying from, you will be nervous at the prospect of leaving home. If you have an especially long flight time, wear comfortable clothes and dress appropriately. Although airline travel is now very casual, remember that your journey may not end at the next stop. You may need to take some form of public transportation to your university or perhaps wait for a transfer. You need to be prepared for this by having on comfortable shoes and clothing that will allow you to transport your own luggage.

Take a few things to do on the airplane, perhaps a book or some music. Almost all flights (especially overseas flights) will have video monitors and an almost constant source of entertainment. I always advise students to take a few snacks, perhaps some granola bars. I have had the unfortunate experience of being served inedible meals on airplanes. If you do too, you may be hungry for quite some time, especially if you have to travel any distance to your university once you arrive. Keep in mind that you should try not to overload your carry on bags, since you will have to get them in and out of the overhead bins. Pack any medications in your carry on and a spare outfit. This will ensure that you have what you need if your suitcase gets lost. If you need any travel medications, like motion sickness or anxiety medication, remember to pack this in the carry-on and to take it early. Try to enjoy your trip; this flight is the start of a great adventure.

Even though you will pack and re-pack and re-think your pre-departure plans a million times before you leave, try to remember that nothing is a disaster unless you lose your passport. Anything that you have forgotten can be sent or bought wherever you end up going. I will generally pack once, rearrange, take some things out, and then close the luggage and not think about it again. I usually will remember some item just when I am too far to go back and get it. But as long as you have your tickets, your passport and some money, you can replace anything.

As the time arrives to leave for your trip, you will be more and more nervous and perhaps busier and busier getting things in order. This is another reason to pack early. It is much easier to do this with a clear head the week before you go and then come back to it in the busy time just before departure to add a few things. Part of this adventure is taking a few things from home, combining them with what you buy abroad, and adding all of the things that one never anticipates needing. These things will keep you busy in your first week, make life interesting as you shop for them, and give you a mission when you are not in classes.

Try to think about the adventure ahead and remember that you will come back to the place that you are leaving. Many students have overwhelming emotions as they leave friends and family. The study abroad experience will be one that can change your life, so leaving the comfort of friends and family is part of this. Try to focus on the good times ahead, new friends, and a whole new view on life and the place that you are going. I often think that the most important thing that people learn while abroad is how much they appreciate all of the people and things that are left behind. You may actually come back to appreciate these people more.

With this in mind pack early and carefully, get on that plane and keep your chin up. Time goes quicker than you will ever imagine and the adventure is just beginning.

Information/ Paperwork Check List

I. COURSE INFORMATION

☐ List of courses that you are or will be registering for

☐ Approval from your home institution for transfer credit for this course (if needed)

☐ Name of the course convener and contact details

II. PRACTICAL INFORMATION

☐ International Office contact information

☐ Accommodation information (including physical address of your accommodation)

☐ If no on campus accommodation, then office of off campus accommodation details

☐ Student association information and other university offered travel information

III. IMMIGRATION INFORMATION

☐ Letter of acceptance on letterhead stationary from your UK university

☐ Copy of recent bank statement

☐ Contact details at your new university for problems or emergencies.

☐ Entry Clearance Form

Packing Guide

I. Household/ Dorm Room Items
- ☐ Towels
- ☐ Adapters
- ☐ Small Appliances (hairdryer, etc)
- ☐ Laptop
- ☐ Travel toothpaste/ toothbrush
- ☐ Travel shampoo/ conditioner
- ☐ Soap

II. Clothing and Outerwear
- ☐ Comfortable shoes
- ☐ Several pairs of jeans/ pants
- ☐ Socks
- ☐ Underclothes
- ☐ T-shirts (long and short sleeved)
- ☐ Sweaters
- ☐ Sweat shirts
- ☐ Shorts
- ☐ Clothes for clubs
- ☐ One nicer outfit (or combination)
- ☐ Jacket, gloves, scarf, hat for winter
- ☐ Lighter jacket for spring/ summer
- ☐ Umbrella
- ☐ Bag/ backpack with zipper

III. Practical Items
- ☐ Alarm Clock
- ☐ Travel document holder
- ☐ Medicine
- ☐ Photo album

IV. Miscellaneous
- ☐ CDs

Chapter 3
Arriving in the UK:
Useful tips for the first weeks

The first two weeks abroad can set the tone for your whole experience. Meet your flat mates, or hall mates, and try to make friends. Attend all of the necessary meetings and a few of the fun events that are arranged for students. If you spend the first couple of weeks either jet lagged or in your room, by the time classes start you may find that others have made friends and have plans that you would have liked to join. Although some students have no difficulty adjusting and are excited to try all of the new events and get into the system, everyone will have doubts and problems. The best way to work through all of these problems and questions is with the help of others, so try to keep this in mind.

Immigration at the Airport:

As mentioned before you will be required to cross Immigration, Passport Control and Customs, when you arrive in the UK. Remember to take the documents with you that I have suggested in chapter one. Also remember to have them handy in your carry-on at Passport Control. When it is your turn to speak with Immigration simply state that you are studying in the UK for the period of time that you plan to attend and give the officer your paperwork.

Some of the questions you may be asked are:

- What is your reason for coming to the UK?
- How long will you be in the UK?
- Where will you be living?
- Are you intending to work in the UK?
- How much money do you have? You may be asked to prove you have enough money with bank statements.
- Do you have any known medical problems?

Answer the questions with short and to the point responses. A long line of people will be behind you and the official will not have time to hear your life story.

After November 13, 2003, the UK requires students who plan to stay in the country for longer than six months to acquire UK entry clearance. This is a form that you need before you get to Immigration and it can be applied for via the British Consulate. For more information go to the website at www.BritainUSA.com/visas/visas. You must get this document before you enter the UK if you plan to stay for longer than six months.

Once you are through Immigration, you will be required to collect you luggage and pass through Customs. You will probably have nothing to declare, but review customs rules before making this decision. Once you pass Customs, you are through the airport and on to your university.

Before you leave the US, you need to determine if your university offers a pick up or "meet and greet" service. This may help you decide on an arrival date. If they do not provide this, ask if they can give you details on how to get to the university. This can be one of the most frustrating things for new students, as many are not used to the fast pace of large cities or taking public transportation. If you must make your way yourself, then I urge you to take your time and ask for as much help as you need. The airports will have information desks that can give advice and point you in the right direction.

Have a plan. This is where any information you have from the university will be useful. If you are planning to take a taxi, remember to have the physical address of where you are going to show to the driver. Black cabs in London are the official taxis. Private individuals or mini cabs are not allowed to operate at the London airports. Always go to the taxi rank to take a taxi and never go with anyone that may approach you in the terminal with the offer of being cheaper. These individuals will almost certainly be unlicensed drivers. The university will be able to tell you about the typical fare from nearby airports and may recommend a taxi company in advance so you could arrange to have one waiting for you. This may also be cost effective if there is a small group of up to three of you trying to get to the same university.

Arriving at Your University:

Whether you have been met and accompanied back to your university or you have found your own way there, many people are surprised when they finally arrive. If you are staying in university accommodations this may shock you as well.

One aspect of universities in the UK is that most are older, and their buildings reflect this as well, and another is that many of the buildings were probably not built originally to be used as a university. You will on occasion find brand new buildings and classrooms that were built for this use, but I have attended classes and taught in buildings that were once houses, churches, flats, and even had an office in an old bedroom! This is part of what gives these universities their charm. It may also mean that your accommodation may be in older condition or circumstance. I have seen reactions from students that range from joy to tears. Remember that the long journey may make you feel better or worse about the situation than it really is, and in general students who were disappointed at first glance have been happy once they have had some sleep and time to adjust.

Many universities have updated accommodations and some have relatively new living quarters. If you are living on campus then you may either have catered or self catering rooms. A catered room gives you a meal plan and access to food prepared at the university. Most of these types of halls of residence also have some small cooking facilities. If you are in self catered accommodation, you will share a kitchen with a number of students, where you will be expected to prepare your meals.

In addition to the older buildings and accommodations, you will find a bookshop, libraries, all sorts of offices and departments, religious gathering places such as chapels or muslin prayer rooms, and a bar or two. The fact that most universities in the UK have bars attached to them is a curiosity for US students, especially when alcohol is banned from most US universities. Not only are there bars on campus, but they may well be the best priced! Remember that in the UK the pubs are ways of community gathering and social time. Even if you are not a drinker, you may find yourself in the bar/ pub spending time with friends. You can always have non alcoholic options such as soft drinks and juices.

You university may be self-contained on one campus, or you may have to travel between sites. It is not uncommon for universities to be quite a distance from their accommodations. Remember that many of the buildings where you study have been there much longer than your university anticipated housing hundreds of students.

Jet Lag

The time change in the UK may be anywhere from five to twelve hours for you. Your overseas flight will almost certainly be overnight and a long journey. Although the time schedule of the flight is overnight it may actually mean that you miss a night of sleep. This time change, in combination with the stress, excitement, and anxiety of arriving may make shifting over to your new time seem insurmountable. There are a few tips that generally work to help students when they arrive.

Helpful hints are to drink as much water on the airplane as possible to stay hydrated. Try to sleep on the plane if possible; even a few hours will help you when you arrive. Once there, try to stay awake, you can do this by taking a shower, a walk, exploring your new area, and if possible getting into the sun when you arrive helps your body adjust to the new time zone. Once you are required to start activities in the morning then you will be forced to get over your jet lag, but try to start off on the right foot.

The best remedy for jet lag is to always try and stay awake the day that you arrive. Although this may mean that you are awake for twenty four hours or more, it will be worth it. When you arrive, have a shower to help wake you up. If you are sleepy, try to have a brisk walk and tour you local area. If you must sleep, only take a short nap and remember to set your alarm clock. Sleep for only a few hours in the afternoon and then remain awake as long as you can into the evening. Once you have reached the evening hours, you can retire for a much needed first night's sleep. Obviously all of this will be easier if you can rest on the plane ride to the UK; but, if this isn't possible, try to stay awake on your arrival day.

Another good technique is to start turning yourself around the week or two before you leave. If you figure the time difference between your home and the UK, and start to go to bed one hour earlier each night and get up one hour earlier each morning, you will to start the process early and in a step by step fashion. You may have trouble going to bed earlier at first; but, after a few mornings of early rising, it will be no problem. You may eventually be getting up for your breakfast in the middle of the night while the rest of your family and room mates sleep, but this is the time you will need to be on once you arrive. This technique is valuable if you are going on a short term study aboard program or must start immediately after you arrive. Although it may be strange to try this at home it does work. Also try to eat meals at new meal times rather than when you feel hungry.

The most important thing about jet lag is not whether you start fighting it before you leave or when you arrive, but being committed to getting over it. I have seen students who will sleep all day and stay awake all night without ever changing to UK time. If you intend on living and studying in another country, you will need to adjust. Some students find that the jet lag is an excuse not to interact with difficult circumstances or the unhappiness about their new situation. I can assure you that these problems will not go away by sleeping through your days.

Getting Settled In

After finding out where your accommodations are, meeting the new people with whom you now live, and exploring your area, there are some other things that you may need to get done to start off your university stay. You will more than likely need to register for classes, attend an orientation session (in the autumn there is fresher's week), and any other activities to get to know the other students, and, of course, classes.

Before arrival you should be informed of times when you need to register and if there is an orientation session. If you have not been informed of this, it is imperative to find out. You can ask your international officer for this information. I also suggest that in this first week at the university that you speak with your professors or course conveners. This is information you should have written down or taken from the prospectus that you were sent. These people can help review your classes, provide room and time information, and ease your worries about taking courses in another country. You may get a feel for how the class runs and the professor's personality as well.

In addition to meeting your professors, you may want to visit with the international office of your university. This is probably the group that will hold an orientation for international students. But remember to check, because there are also university wide orientations for new students. The international center can also put you into touch with student groups or provide information on trips and activities planned for the year or semester. Most will operate some short day trips and other functions. Find these and register for them early, as they are generally much less expensive than taking a train and less hassle for travel. Registering early is also a good idea if you do not yet know other students to travel with. Be patient though, in the first weeks of term the international office will be teeming with new students and activities.

If you arrive for the autumn semester you may well be involved with an activity called Fresher's Week. A Fresher is the equivalent to a freshman in the US, and the week before classes start normally you will see a flurry of activities at the university and associated bars, clubs, and pubs to welcome students. These activities will range from very organized university events to show off student groups and special events to the absolutely mad nights out at the local clubs and pubs or the university student union. I encourage people to attend even if they are not inclined to the wilder side of the events. This is a typical UK university event and one that may open your eyes to student life and university culture. It will also provide years of stories. Many people find that they need a week to rest after Fresher's week, so you may want to be selective in what you attend. After all, the end of fresher's week marks the beginning of classes.

The first day of classes in the UK is generally the first day of lecture and work. You need to go prepared and ready to take notes. Many times I have seen students from the US await their syllabus and then make a quick exit. As the semesters are short in the UK and the lecturers need to get material covered, you will start with lecture the first day. Have your supplies ready and be prepared to work hard from day one.

Other Possibilities for the First Weeks

As every country in the UK has different regulations, different universities will require different things of you. Use this as a general overview of ideas. Remember to check with your individual university for an exact list of what you must complete before classes start.

Some tasks that you may have to complete include registering your passport, registering with police (when necessary), getting library accounts sorted, and obtaining student identification cards. You may also want to get an International Student Identity Card for additional discounts and a youth rail card if you will ride the trains or other public transport frequently. We will discuss this more in the chapter on UK travel.

Depending on the country where you are studying, you may need to go to the police department and register your passport. Check with the university international office about this. If you do need to register the passport, you simply take it to the local police station with a photograph; but, you must leave it for as long as two weeks so do not plan any travel out of the country at this time. If you must make an emergency trip abroad, go directly to the police station and explain the circumstances in order to retrieve your passport.

At your university you will need a student identification card. At some universities these also work as library cards, but some are required to be validated as library cards. You may need to check with the library to get this done. Some times these identification cards serve to allow entry to different buildings if your university is secured. You may need a meal card as well if you are in catered accommodation. Clarify your meal plan so that you can plan for the meals that are not provided or times when the meal facilities are closed.

Another card that you may want to get is an International Student Identity Card (ISIC) issued by the International Student Travel Confederation. You will need this card to buy student travel fairs and to get discounts at many retailers. The card is worth having as many cinemas, travel and tour operators, museums, historic sights, and other businesses give student discounts. You can buy the card before you leave or when you are abroad. If your airfare is a student fare, then you may have to have one before you leave. The advantage of having these identity cards is that they are universally recognized, while your own university identification card may not qualify you for discounts.

Youth cards are available for travel on the rail system and other public transport. If you use this service often, these cards may be worth the investment. Many of these cards are paid up front and then you can use a discount for the allotted time. We will discuss these further in the chapter on travel in the UK. If you do decide that you will use this card, the first two weeks in the UK is the time to purchase it.

Budget

Making a budget is a very important idea in the first two weeks. Therefore it should be a top priority. Your UK institute or your home university may have made suggestions for the amount of extra money to bring with you, it is sometimes impossible to tell what you will need until you arrive. It may be unfeasible to budget for the things for your flat until you arrive, as you do not know what has been provided or the state of what is available. Further, most people underestimate what they will need in terms of spending money during their time away. With the nightlife that I have spoken about earlier in the chapter, many students find that they have not anticipated for the amount of activity that is taking place.

Another reason that a budget is important is the fact that you must make your money last the entire time that you are abroad. This may mean weeks, but sometimes means months or years. Without a budget it may be easy to spend quite a bit upfront and have nothing left for the end of term, which is often when you will have more parties and commitments with friends before you leave. I have seen students spend the majority of their money within the first half of their study abroad experience and then find themselves forced to forego many end of term events and bargain shop for gifts and souvenirs.

In budgeting for your time abroad, you need to remember that the beginning and the end of the time will be the most expensive. When you arrive you will need to buy personal items, groceries, items for your room, your flat, and many other comfort items. Upon leaving you may have packing and shipping charges, extra luggage, need to buy gifts or souvenirs, attend going away functions, and other events. The time in between may be quite routine, with a budget for food, entertainment, local travel, sightseeing, and meals at restaurants.

The other large expense in your budget is any travel that you want to do. The UK is a base for European travel (see Chapter 7) and, although you may be able to spend little on each airfare, train fare, hostels, and food, it still can add up quickly. Each trip will have some hidden costs, like getting to the airport, and some budget flights are at airports that you must take a train to get to. Adding a train fair can cost the same amount as the ticket itself. Also most travel involves the costs of sightseeing once you arrive at your destination and travel within the destination city itself, to and from the airport and around from sight to sight. Even public transportation fares can add up over a weekend.

I would suggest having two budgets: a travel budget and a living expense budget. I would allot more money for the first and last weeks of the time abroad and try to find a balance in the middle weeks. Attempt to follow your costs for groceries, bills, transportation, supplies, and other necessary items. This will help you with an idea of what you must spend weekly and what you have left over for entertainment. Try to stay on budget for your fixed costs and within reason for entertainment. Some weeks may be busier and have more to offer than others, so this may be adjusted as the semester continues.

Your travel budget should include a top ten list of places you would like to go. In your free time you can look for what is affordable within this range. This may help you prioritize your destinations. Some places are very inexpensive to get to at all times, whereas some other popular destinations are always expensive.

Compare this list with friends and flat mates, as you will need to find travel partners. Not only is it easier to travel in a group or pairs, but the expense of food and rooms can be shared. Then you can match these ideas to your travel budget to see how far you can go. This may take some negotiation with others as everyone will have different ideas and standards, but try to stay within this allotted budget. Remember the hidden expenses and try to be realistic. I would also recommend to you only book one trip at a time, as traveling with others may help you learn who you can and can not travel with as well as give you good ideas for the next trip.

Whether you decide to make your budget as suggested in chapter eleven or follow your own guidelines, keep an eye on your spending and make the amount you have go as far as possible. Although some students feel that the opportunity is worth some debt, and in some cases it may be, remember that this may be a burden when you return to your home country. As with any budget the best advice is to set a limit and try to stay within it unless there are very compelling reasons not to.

Jobs

If you have a student visa because you will study more than three months in the UK, then you are eligible to work for twenty hours a week during the semester and more during the summer. You need to check for these ever changing regulations at the UK Home Office, but most students do work in the UK if they are there for an extended length of time. Some students who are in the UK for a semester only will decide against getting a job, as many have saved beforehand for the time abroad. This is a very personal decision, and one that needs to be weighed against your financial situation, your coursework, and goals for the time abroad. However, working abroad will also make you more a part of the community in which you live.

If you do decide that you wish to work while studying, then the most important thing is to look for a job early. Many of the jobs that students generally find, such as restaurants, pubs, and small shops, are taken quickly once all of the students arrive. You can look either in your university's career center, newspaper, or on advertisement boards, through local newspapers, or for signs in the widows on the shops. I would encourage students to work within walking distance of their accommodations if possible, as some restaurants and pubs will have late hours and there may be little or no public transportation.

Once you have applied and been hired for a job, you will need your employer to write a letter saying that they are willing hire you, the hours, and the pay for the job. You take this letter to the benefits office (you can check for the local office) for a National Insurance Card. This will give you a legal number to work and also allow the government to monitor the taxes that you pay out of your wages. Once you have this number your employer can complete the necessary forms and get you started in your new position.

Some students find working their only means of survival, while others find the work a way to make friends and see another side of their study country. If your first language is not English, then this will be a very good opportunity to practice with a variety of people. The only caution is to make sure that working does not pull you away from your studies and jeopardize your academics. Keep in mind that many opportunities in the study abroad experience may not fit your work schedule, so you may have to give up some opportunities that other students can take advantage of, such as university events and day trips. It is a personal choice, and one that only you can make about your time abroad.

An Emotional Time

Even though you may be excited about your adventure abroad, it is an emotional time for many. Away from family and friends, in a strange new place, with mixed emotions about your accommodation, and the frustration of working within a system that you do not understand may cause some doubts.

You may find that you are sad because you have left family, a boyfriend, or a girlfriend. You may worry what this time abroad will do to these relationships. The time abroad can strengthen them or cause you to reexamine them. Remember that you will change during this time, whether you intend to or not. The experiences that you have may make bonds stronger or more difficult. If you have left a boyfriend or girlfriend, you may find that it is difficult for them to understand your new surroundings, new friends, and new lifestyle. Perhaps understanding this and speaking about it ahead of time will help. You can spend time before you leave planning for their visits and time to speak on the phone and e-mail. Try to focus on the time you have on your program and these other relationships will work out for the best. I have seen many students spend nights on the telephone to home while others are out having fun. Although this may be how you choose to spend your time, you may be missing out on the only time you have abroad to experience the culture and nightlife. Try to be flexible and hope that the people in your life can understand this incredible opportunity that you have.

Many students find themselves lonely when they arrive. It may be some time between your orientation and the start of class. Try to attend any and all functions offered and to make friends with your flat mates. From my experience almost everyone has a flat mate or two who will try to be friendly and take you out to meet people or involve you in activities. If you continually say that you aren't interested in participating, people will stop asking. Making a friendship network is one of the most important things to do. You will need friends in tough times and in good times, and they are what makes the experience that much easier and memorable. Be active and be involved. You will never meet people if you stay in your room!

Even if you are not sad or lonely in your first weeks, you will almost certainly be confused. In a new country it is easy to get lost, to not understand people and how to do things, and to be uncertain about things at your new university. Don't be too hard on yourself during this time. If you ask around you will find most people are confused or were at the beginning of their studies. Gather as much information as you can. Keep asking questions. Your support network will help. Eventually you will figure most things out, or at least learn to live with a bit of confusion. At any university the beginning of term is the most puzzling time, so try to get through the first weeks and things will improve.

This chapter has attempted to help you understand what you will be going through a bit more thoroughly, to give some hints about settling in, and most of all to encourage you to stick these first weeks out. I have seen many students who wanted to leave once they have arrived (and a few have). I can assure you that all students go through times like this and living and studying abroad is a demanding thing to do. Take one day at a time and soon enough you will be giving advice to others.

Chapter 4
Academics

The United Kingdom has an entirely different system of studying than the United States. Although the different countries of the UK vary in their educational systems, many of the elements remain the same. In many years of working with study abroad students, I believe that one of the main problems with exchanges is the fact that students are not prepared for the new educational system before they arrive. When they do arrive, they try to conceptualize the system based on their knowledge of their own educational system, particularly those students from the US. The two systems may seem similar, and may be in some ways, but this is a pitfall for students. If you approach the education in the UK with the same perception as the US, it may result in a difficult journey.

To understand university in the UK, it is important to talk generally about the system. Historically universities have been available only to a very small percentage of the population in the UK, whereas a significant portion of American students have attended university in the US. It is difficult to get into university in the UK and requires a tremendous amount of preparation, so in this way students arriving in their first year are the equivalent of juniors in the United States. In the UK students study particular subject areas from the ages of 16 to 18 in order to gain entry into university. These subjects determine what you can study at the university, unlike the US where students have all options open and can easily change from subject to subject.

Students in the UK normally attend for three years (this is different in Scotland where an undergraduate degree can be four years). The first year is a foundation year in which students generally study the more basic levels of their subject. Years two and three are more concentrated and at a higher level. A student must pass each year to be admitted to the next, and students have more than one opportunity to take exams and resubmit essays in order to pass classes.

Understanding the academic structure may help with the study abroad process. Universities will have a rector instead of a president, a course convener instead of a chair of a department, and the registrar's department may be called a registry. Besides the different names used, many are divided into schools under larger university titles. These schools are a collection of similar academic courses and are largely run within themselves. The core academic structure and offices, such as finance, libraries, registry, and bookshops, run to support the schools. Schools are generally commanded by a Head of School who meets regularly with the course conveners who pass information to the lecturers. Although different universities are organized in different ways (some into colleges like Oxford and others into campuses) a general hierarchy exists at each with the rector or vice-chancellor in the top position.

In regards to courses, the numbers and descriptions can be misleading. If in doubt about course levels, try and contact the lecturer via e-mail and get more detailed information. Sometimes students think that if they enroll in a first year class it will be exceptionally easy. Though it may well be true for some, it is a higher level than a freshman course in the United States simply due to the fact that students in the UK are more prepared for university.

Another difference is that most students in the UK think of university as a full time job. With a changing financial structure for the UK and higher education, more and more students have had to seek part time work, but many will not work as they attend university. This makes the work at university more like a job, where classes can be thought of as meeting with a boss with time away from these meetings for individual work and preparation. So while you may believe that that attending lectures is enough work, courses do require an intense amount of work outside the classroom.

Educational success eludes many students when they study abroad. Some of this is due to false expectations and some is due to lack of understanding and preparation. Many students expect the level of work to be similar to their home universities, and it may well be, but most find it more intense and more self guided. There are also many pitfalls along the way. But as long as you take the work seriously and try to avoid common mistakes, you will be fine. Remember the university probably offers numerous services to help, such as reading and writing centers, testing centers, libraries, and computer help, so take advantage of them.

Titles

Although most of your teachers in the UK may have PhDs, most are not referred to as Doctor, where in the United States this is standard practice. Most of your teachers will have the title of lecturer, although this may be distinguished by other titles such as senior lecturer, or other higher levels as well. The highest level that a lecturer can reach is a professor. When one is made a professor he or she has reached a high pinnacle in their career and are recognized as an expert in the field. If you have a lecturer that is a professor, it is polite to call them professor rather than Doctor, as this is a higher title. Most others will give you information on their preferred titles in their syllabus or on the first day of class.

Classes

Classes in the UK are typically not mandatory. You may find that your lecturers do take roll but will sometimes send letters or e-mails when you do not attend. Some will pass around registers for you to sign at the beginning or end of class. For the most part, attendance is not as strict as in the US. Many American students find this a pitfall. As they learn that classes are not mandatory, they find themselves attending fewer and fewer. Like any other university that you have attended, the material covered in the classroom generally has relevance for the exam, essay, or assignments that you are asked to complete, so it is in your favor to attend.

Many classes will only require one piece of work for your grade, such as an essay or final exam. For many US students who are used to averaging grades throughout a semester, this can be difficult. On the outside it seems that missing classes is fine as there are not weekly assignments and grades. Be aware that the lecturers do remember who has attended and are likely to grant more leniencies to those who are there and make an effort.

In many circumstances, UK classes are taught as lecture only and students are not permitted to speak or ask questions until a tutorial or a question time at the end of class. This varies from university to university and lecturer to lecturer. I would suggest following the model of the class, but be aware in strict lecture circumstances that lecturer will not allow interruptions or questions. If your class has a tutorial then this will be the time in which there is interaction with the lecturer and the material.

Lectures and classes in the UK are not designed to be the only source of information on a topic. They are often times to discuss specific works, topics of interest, or lecturer's work. Most syllabi will have extensive reading lists and you will be expected to have looked at these sources, even if they are never mentioned in class. Lectures are a small fraction of the work that is expected from a student. The work load is generally said to be that every ten hours you spend in lecture should be the equivalent to 100 hours of work outside the classroom. Lecturers will expect that you are studying outside of class, even if you are not tested on this until the final exam or essay.

Assessment

As mentioned previously, most classes are assessed through one or a few pieces of work. Sometimes this one exam or essay will be your entire grade, so doing poorly on it is not an option. Most classes are assessed either through essay, exam, or a combination of both. Many American students find that they do not do well on these assessments as they are so different from what they are used to. Rarely, if ever, have I seen a multiple choice test used, and never a true/false test. Even if you do take an exam, it is more than likely to be in an essay format.

Essays

If you are asked to write an essay, the professor will give you a title, although in some cases the students are tasked with creating their own essay titles from their own area of interest. Most likely you will be given a list to choose from, and the topics will follow the course content. You will also be expected to incorporate the outside class reading and research that you are doing independently. If you are looking for advice or clarification, try to ask early as the material you may need to clarify questions and issues can be in a variety of places.

All of the material that you will need, and that your teacher recommends, will be in your university's library. Many students in the UK do not buy textbooks. Instead the books are bought in larger number for holding in the library, where they are available. Be warned, if you wait until the last minute to do work, then the books you need are the same books all of the other class members need too.

Essays are generally assigned to be a certain length, based on word count rather than the number of pages. An average word count for an essay is 2000 to 3000 words. Sometimes you will write fewer and some courses will require more. More than 3000 words is generally an extended essay. It is important to think of it as word count as the paper used in the UK is a different size to that in the US. The paper in the UK is standard A4 size, slightly longer and narrower than the US standard letter size paper, which is 8 1/2 x 11". (You need to be mindful of this as well if you are taking work back to the US to submit at a later time.) A general rule in writing essays is that the word limit is fixed, but you can deviate plus or minus ten percent. This may help you when putting your work together, but try to stay near the word limit so not to lose points.

In writing an essay the best advice that I can give students is that they need to write a paper that makes an argument, answers a question with convincing material support, or creates a narrative. The descriptive type papers that most American universities require will not get very good marks. Essays are more than giving material back to the lecturer that they suggested to you, but taking all of those readings, articles, journals and crafting ideas about them. The most common type of essay question will ask you to use the literature and other sources to take a stand on an issue one way or another. Essays may also ask you to discuss ideas, theories, texts, major works, and lectures.

If you are asked in an essay to discuss an issue or a quote or sentence, which is a common format, then you must take information surrounding that idea and either support it or provide information to show why the statement, idea, or quote is valid or invalid. In this way the question is more than just a true or false issue, or more than agreement on the topic; but one that asks you to take materials that have been suggested by the lecturer, perhaps some ideas from the lecture, and then go further. You must put them together in a way that will actually discuss the topic. This is more than a repetition of notes, journals, and books, and is designed to show what you have learned and what you think about an issue. It is not to provide a synopsis of what others have said.

Many times you will be asked to compare and contrast two issues, themes, events, or topics. This is one of the easier essays to write, although many people tend to ignore the directions. If you are asked to compare and contrast then you will need to write about how these two things are similar and how they are different. The two may not be obvious to you at first, which is where further research will be needed. This comes back to the basic element of an essay: your own argument. Perhaps you are asked to compare and contrast so that you have to look further into an issue to see these similarities and differences. How do the basic ideas presented in the course lead you to these conclusions? How do the fundamentals of your subject come into play on this issue? When you start to look further than the texts and journals, that is where you should be writing. Essays are about taking a large amount of information that informs a subject, reading it, analyzing it and then using all of it in the final product.

In every essay that you write, you must also have good references and many of them. Ideas and theses about topics cannot be formed by only reading one or two books or articles. You must bring together a variety of authors and their works. You should also check with your professor to make sure that you are following referencing guidelines. Some universities will issue these in a style guide, while others will use more nationally and internationally recognized systems. Check with your lecturer early to see about the style guide for your essay. Nothing looks less professional than asking a day ahead of the due date.

Writing an essay is very difficult to do well. In order to gather all the material that you need and to effectively answer the questions being asked you should expect to do hours of research. This research is really only half of the work. Once you have done the research and collected it together in an organized fashion, you must come to conclusions about the material yourself and present them in a clear and concise fashion. This is the part that can take some time to finish.

I once wrote an essay for a class in the UK, for which I was awarded a reasonable, but not great, mark. When I asked the professor where I went wrong, he answered that I had not written an essay. I was confused by this until he went on to explain to me that what I had done was "prepared" to write an essay. I had volumes of material and had been reading the correct texts. I had even put other's ideas into a concise and correct summary. The professor explained to me that this was only half of writing an essay, the part I should have done early in the term and thought about to make my own ideas and an argument. I had failed to take my own advice on this matter. To write a good essay you must go further than other authors. You must incorporate your learning into the essay and should display not only your ability to research but your ability to think about this research.

Exams

Exams are typically given after a course has ended and after a week or two of study time. They are not given in the same classroom you meet in for lecture, but in large lecture halls where you may have many students taking different tests at the same time. Your lecturer may not be present at the exams, but instead there will be invigilators who will proctor the tests. Exams are very formal situations when you are not allowed to leave the room without a chaperone. I have even had to chaperone people to the restroom when I was invigilating.

Most exams are typically essay format but some can be short answer, depending on the subject. Exams are taken at the end of the term and most students never see the written tests again, but merely their grade once posted. I would advise students to take exams very seriously, as they may make up your entire grade and, in some cases, determine your ability to continue at the university. Do not be late, even if it means arriving too early. There is never any talking permitted and the exam environment is very stern.

Students are often very nervous about taking exams, with good reason. The key to being less nervous and doing well is being prepared. First, be prepared for the situation. Eat something before you go, get a good night's sleep, be early, have pens, pencils, a picture identification card, and other things you may need (like a calculator, ruler, etc.) depending on the subject.

The second way to be prepared is to have completed an ample amount of study and preparation for the exam itself. Most lecturers offer a review session or will give hints about the exam in the last class session. Most old exams are available for review either through the school or at the library. It is worth the time to go and review these. Even if the questions change significantly, which they generally do not, it will help to know the type of questions that the lecturers asks. My advice to students is to try and write one of these old exams as if it were the test. It will give you an idea of how much you can write in the time allotted and how difficult it is to put ideas together clearly in a test circumstance.

Preparation for exams is like writing an essay in many ways. You must try and read a variety of material and you must also try and put these ideas together. Studying for these exams is not something that can be done in a cram session. You should start studying well before the exam date and study a little each day. If you review the texts, key concepts, and start a study sheet/guide for questions that you think may appear on the exam, you will not be as panicked at the end. I would advise students to start from an early date making outlines of important issues and points in the class and from class notes and readings. Then, once it is exam time, you will be prepared and this will lessen the stress of the actual exam day.

Grades

After you have submitted an exam or essay, it may take months to receive a grade for this piece of work. Unlike the United States where one teacher has the ability to grade a paper or test and give a mark, in the UK the papers and exams have to pass through a variety of people. Once your initial lecturer has marked all of the papers/exams, a sample must be sent to another lecturer at the same university. This is called second marking. All of the papers that have very good or very poor grades must be double checked, as well as a sample of exams from the middle. Once the second marker has checked these grades, and the grades altered based on his/her recommendations, another sample will go to an external marker. An external marker is someone at a completely different university who teaches the same subject. This marker then can monitor the quality of work and grades compared to other institutions in the UK. This system verifies that a lecturer is using the right criteria for marking, in which all passing marks and exceptional marks are awarded based on merit and not on favoritism or dislike.

Although the grading scale in the UK runs from zero to one hundred, similar to the US, the difference is that they do not use the top of the scale. My advice to students when looking at their UK grades to decide if they are good is to add about twenty five points to convert it to the US scale. In this case if you received a 60 on a paper in the UK, it would be the equivalent to an 85 in the US.

In the UK a 70 is a very good score, and one that is difficult to get, so don't expect to get A's even on very good papers and exams. I have seen many students who received sixties on papers and were disappointed. A sixty in the UK is a good score (remember that rarely will anyone make the equivalent to an American "A" score.).

Grade Reference Table

UK Grade	Equivalent US grade
70	95
60	85
50	75
40	65
35 This is generally the lowest passing grade	50
30	55

Time Tables, Schedules, and Calendars

Most UK universities will start in late September or early October. The semester generally runs for twelve weeks with a Christmas break. Some universities will finish all exams before this break while others will have exams after the Christmas holidays. The spring semester sees classes starting in February and ending in June, with exams in this time also. This semester is twelve weeks also, but most universities will have an Easter break from two weeks to one month in March or April, depending when Easter falls, when there are no classes taught. Universities in the UK typically do not have summer courses. There are exceptions to all of these schedules, particularly if you are doing a more applied course, such as teaching or nursing. Check with your individual university for exact semester dates.

Academic Pitfalls

Many students who come for study abroad find that academics may rank low on their lists once they arrive. Many institutions will only transfer grades as pass or fail marks, so the consequences do not affect their grade point averages. Many students simply find the vibrant nightlife and the availability of things to do on campus, such as student union activities or a night at the school pub, too much of a distraction. I understand that it is up to each individual student to decide where priorities lie while they are abroad. I can't say that I only did academics while I was studying abroad, but I was forced to do more than many students I have since seen. This is a balance only you can decide on, but remember to do well in this environment you will need to take the work seriously.

Some of the most common pitfalls for students are not attending classes, not preparing enough for essays and exams, and the expectation that the coursework will be the same as their home country. Even though you may not be required to attend classes in the UK, it is important to go when possible. These classes are your roadmap to the material. I have rarely seen students who attended no classes do well on the exam or essay, although I have offered this option to students every year. Also, classes are good places to make friends and learn about culture. You may hate the course material, but seeing the lecture format is a cultural experience itself.

The other pitfall that students find is that they expect for grading to be the same as their home institute. Perhaps you are used to having many assessments so you can average the good and the not so good grades into a reasonable average grade. This just isn't the case in the UK. Students may also feel that the quality of the work that they would have done at home is good enough for this different system. While this may be true, the work done in American universities is often at a lower level and more descriptive. This may be the first time you have been asked to put forth your opinion and defend it, so take the opportunity.

Ultimately it is your decision on how your time is best spent. I think a balance between work and play is needed, but this means a fifty percent /fifty percent exchange, not the ten percent /ninety percent partnership between work and play that I have seen many students strike. Some of the work that you do while abroad may be the best that you have produced and you may be very proud of having completed it.

Chapter 5
Living in the UK

There are no complete culture guides to the UK, and one reason for this is that it would be impossible to explain everything. Because this guide is different than most, I have decided to try and explain some of the more confusing aspects of living in the UK, as well as things that you will use on a regular basis. Use this as a key to understanding some of the institutions that you may interact with such as the post office, bank, and the doctor. We will consider things to do at the post office, what to do when you are sick, grocery stores, restaurants and pubs, and also some American restaurants that you may find helpful when you are homesick. The chapter then concludes with 30 helpful hints about the UK, that may come in handy when trying to negotiate the culture. This is followed by Dr. H's tips, a lighthearted explanation of how not to act in the UK!

Useful Places
The Post Office

The post office is an obvious choice for an important place, as most people will be sending letters and packages home; however, in the UK people use the post office for many other things. Depending on your living situation, you may need to use the post office to pay bills, buy a TV license, get a driver's permit, and of course, send correspondence. One aspect of the post office that surprises many Americans is the numerous services that it offers. In the UK the post office does everything from postage stamps, mail letters, bill payment, social security and other benefit payments, foreign exchange, insurance for travel and automobiles, and paperwork for many services. So don't be surprised to see people walk up to the post office window and actually receive money rather than pay for something.

If you live in a flat where you receive bills for gas, electricity, water, or other services, you can pay these bills at the post office. The post office only accepts cash and UK personal checks and will generally charge a small fee. If you do not have a check book or are collecting money from many people, this can be the easiest way to pay. Simply take your bill to the window and the teller will give you the charge amount. If you wish to avoid the fee, you can take the bill to the bank of the company that issued the bill and pay it there.

If you have a television in the UK, you are required to buy a TV license. Public television stations are run by the state – namely the BBC. These stations have no commercials, so they are supported by license fees. You must buy a license even if you do not intend to watch these stations; by merely turning on the TV you are liable for this tax. Inspectors will check if you have a license and will fine you if you do not. You can buy the license for one year or on a month-by-month basis, the easiest option if you will not be there for a whole year. Forms are available at the post office, or online. Be aware that there is a fine of up to £1000 if you are caught with a television but without a television license.

You can buy postage stamps at the checkout stands of many bookshops, news shops, and grocery stores. There are two types of mail in the UK; first class and second class. Although both are delivered relatively quickly, first class gets a greater priority with over 90% being delivered by the next day. If you plan to mail letters outside of the UK, you can buy a booklet of worldwide postage stamps at retail stores, as well as a booklet of worldwide postcard stamps. Doing so will save you from waiting at the post office, especially if you are purchasing just stamps. Any oversize letters or packages will need to be taken to the post office and weighed. You will also need to go to the post office for any specialty stamps (which are generally issued about every month) or collector's items such as coins.

The Bank

If you plan to stay in the UK for an extended period of time, you may need a UK bank account. As a student these are relatively easy to get. Once again you will need to go to the bank itself and bring your passport and letter from your UK university confirming your student status and address where you live, as well as an initial deposit. A student account will then be opened for you and a card issued. If you can, request access to a debit card, called a Switch or Delta card in the UK as this is very useful. Otherwise all of your transactions will be in cash. Checks are rarely used in stores although most stores will accept them and require a check card (a debit card usually doubles as this too) which guarantees the check up to a certain amount. If your debit card is not a check card also, checks will be useless to you in stores and can only be used to pay bills.

If you are only in the UK for a short period of time most people use their ATM/Visa debit card from the US. Most bank machines and stores will accept them and you will have access to cash. You can also use credit cards in most stores. Which ever method you use, credit or debit cards, remember to sign the back of the card as retailers will check your signature on the card and on paper as a measure of identification. They will not accept a card that has not been signed without more identification. The UK is in the process of switching to a PIN system for credit and debit cards for purchases in stores, but you will probably find that you have to sign for purchases bought using a US card.

The Doctor/ National Health Service

Students who are in the UK for over six months are eligible for services from the National Health Service. Students who are there for a shorter period of time will be treated in emergencies, but asked to pay for services that they use. If you are involved in an accident or need emergency treatment, you will be treated regardless of your student status. Most students are lucky enough to survive the time abroad with little more than a bad cold, but you need to be prepared just in case. If you are in the UK for over a year, you will want to register with a general practitioner. This is the doctor or clinic that you will contact when you are ill. Otherwise your university may provide a health clinic or physician's office that will see you in an emergency.

When you do not feel well in the UK start at the pharmacist, or call a doctor for advice. In the UK health care advice can be given by pharmacy technicians and pharmacists and many more medicines are available over the counter. You can go to the neighborhood pharmacy and they will recommend medicines for you or suggest seeing a physician if they cannot help. If you feel that you need antibiotics then it is best to go to the physician first, as pharmacies cannot give these without prescriptions. If you do need a doctor, try your university health service. Most provide, at least, the services of a nurse and can make referrals. You may have to wait to be seen, but appointments are generally given within forty-eight hours. If you are too unwell to go to the clinic, a doctor can make a house call in some cases.

If you do see a physician and are given a prescription, it can be filled at a local pharmacy. All prescriptions are charged at a flat rate, so there will be no surprises when it comes to paying. You can ask at the pharmacy if you have any questions about the medicine, as this is also one of their duties.

Many students find that physicians in the UK are more reluctant to give prescriptions and provide care with little high technology medicine. If you visit the doctor, you may not have blood tests or other tests, but the doctor may still make a diagnosis and prescribe medicine. Health care in the UK, rather than providing on the basis of the ability to pay, is provided at a certain level for all citizens and visitors, such as students. I always try to think of trips to the doctor as an opportunity to think about differences in the cultures. Remember that you are a guest in the country and need to be respectful of different ways of doing some things. Just because your experience is different from the US, it doesn't mean that you have not received high quality care.

Eating in the UK

When talking about eating in the UK we will divide the section into three parts, firstly what to expect when eating in the UK, secondly where to grocery shop and the major differences in shopping and lastly a few tastes of home! Finding the right places to shop and the food you want and need are often complaints of students, as well as the higher costs of restaurants. Being knowledgeable of the differences and what to expect can make the experience much easier to deal with. Although many students complain about the food and restaurant service when they first arrive, they often realize that the differences are both good and make the cultural portion of the trip rewarding.

Restaurants, Pubs, Typical Food, Cost of Food

If you are out for a meal in the UK, you can expect a wide range of food. Although many people may have told you that the food will be bland or not very exciting, the UK offers a huge range of restaurants, catering to different tastes and nationalities. From my experience you can experience more varied type of cuisine, with a lot of fusion from Asia, Europe, and the Americas.

Dining out can be a very different experience from country to country. Traditionally many people do not eat out often in the UK, but this is changing with the younger generation. One reason is the expense associated with the occasion. You will recognize that eating out can be expensive, even at fast food chains or more casual restaurants. One way to try to get around this is to eat early. Most people eat dinner much later in the UK, after having lunch early in the afternoon (1pm) and tea, which generally consists of a cup of tea, cakes or snacks after work hours. Many restaurants will offer special prices for those who come early, sometimes called a pre-theatre meal, which are served between 5:30 and 7pm. A set menu from which you can chose an appetizer (called a starter), a main course, and perhaps a dessert (sometimes called pudding). These choices are typically the same sizes served all night, but much better value for money.

Another common place to eat is the pub. Pubs offer a huge variety of cuisine, with some offering very modern choices. People will typically eat at pubs for lunch as many stop serving food after lunch time and focus on a different clientele. If you do opt for a pub lunch, you can get anything from traditional fish and chips to the very British Ploughman's lunch of cheese and pickle. These dishes are generally good value and can be generous portions. I recommend that everyone try at least one pub lunch while you are abroad. You will find all types of people, from locals to tourists at the pub. Try to avoid pubs in the touristy places, where prices will be higher and quality often not as good. If you are traveling to small towns or villages, pubs can be a real cultural experience as they are the town hub and will be busy with activity and news.

When you do go for a longer meal at perhaps a more formal restaurant you can expect to stay longer, have less service, and pay more than you are used to in the US. Restaurants will charge more, but will be less pushy about getting you out once you have finished eating. It is not uncommon to go out to eat and have pre-dinner drinks, a starter, main courses, dessert, coffees or after dinner liquor, and then stay on and chat. This means that you may be at one restaurant for many hours. Don't expect the wait staff to be at your table every five minutes with refills, hurrying you along with your food and drinks. You will most likely have to ask for these things and wait for the waiters to come by. This is very common and not considered bad service, but simply another way to have a dining experience. You may enjoy, as I did, having the luxury of more conversion and time with friends once I had met them for dinner. It is also an experience to have one really nice meal and the time together in one place rather than finding many places to go or a variety of things to do in one evening.

Grocery Shopping

Although you may shop at small, locally owned stores, you will also have occasion to go to larger chain supermarkets. Most of these big stores are outside of the main shopping districts, but this is not always the case and you may find a local supermarket very close to where you live. As with the US, these larger stores will offer a better selection and greater value. You will still pay more for items than you will be used to, but remember this is true of many things, not only groceries.

Perhaps the biggest difference in grocery shopping is that you not only have to bag your own groceries, but you will most likely have to carry whatever you buy as you won't have a car to drive home in so you must consider your purchases carefully. Many people will only buy groceries for one or two days and visit the store every other day. Some will buy for a longer period of time and take a taxi if possible. Whichever is your plan, make sure that you can carry whatever you have bought.

Several major grocery store chains exist and you may shop at one or more of these depending on your location. I will list some of the major names of supermarkets, so that you will know them when you see them. See the appendix for their web sites.

- Sainsbury's, or sometimes J.S. Sainsbury's, or Sainsbury's Metro (small inner city stores)
- Tesco's, or sometimes Tesco Express
- Safeway
- Sommerfield
- ASDA (owned by Wal Mart)
- Waitrose
- Co-Op (these are generally smaller stores)

A Taste of Home

When you get homesick, there are many items that will ease this homesickness when you can find them. Some items, such as Hershey's bars or other American candy bars will be easy to find in small shops and grocery stores. You will also be able to buy some American products like Betty Crocker cake mixes and frostings, even though they will be very expensive. On occasion you will also see stores that specialize in imported products, such as grape jelly,

American style peanut butter, American cereals, and other cooking supplies. They may also help to get seasonal items if you plan on cooking for Thanksgiving. Of all of the grocery store chains, Waitrose generally has the biggest variety of imported products. You will pay exorbitant prices for many of these imported goods, as much as three times the price for cereal and candy. These items are great to have as a treat, but you also need to try things from your new country and live on the local goods.

If I ever wanted a taste of home I was more likely to go to an American restaurant. You will find many chains all through the UK. Perhaps the most widespread is T.G.I. Fridays. There are other chains, such as the Hard Rock Café, Chiles, and Outback Steakhouse that have restaurants in the UK, but these are fewer. If you live in London or any big city, you will have more choices at your disposal. If you are in a smaller village or town, you may have to take advantage of these when visiting larger cities. I never frown on students visiting these places and having a taste of home. This can be an excellent cure for homesickness or a remedy to help you through a rough spot. You can expect to pay more for the same items you would get at these restaurants, but the taste of home will be worth it.

Useful Tips

Here are 30 tips that may help you understand the daily living experience in the UK.

	Top 30 UK Tips
A & E	If you need to go to an Emergency Room then you actually need to go to A & E (Accident and Emergency) or Casualty as it is sometimes called.
A to Z guides	If you are going to live anywhere for a significant amount of time, you will need an A to Z. These are maps that list every street. If you live in a big city, especially London, this is a "must have" item.
Buying Clothes	Clothing sizes are different in the UK than in the US and in Europe. In the UK you can figure your size for women's clothing by adding the number 4 to your current size

Buying Shoes	(for example, a size 12 would be a 16 in England). Most men's clothes are the same sizes (waist and length measurements). Shoes sizes are also different in the UK. One of the easiest ways to learn your size is to look inside your tennis shoes. Most labels will show US, UK, and European sizes.
Calling Home/ Calling Cards	Many students will bring pre-paid phone cards or phone cards through their local carrier to their university. While this is fine and may work in an emergency, it is almost always better value to buy a pre-paid phone card when you are abroad. You can generally buy these at corner stores and pay only pennies a minute to talk. The best way to choose is to look at convenience store windows, where the rates are generally posted, and find the best rate for the country you are calling.
Cell Phones	Some students prefer to get mobile phones when they arrive in the UK, which give you more freedom when making calls and more privacy. You will generally be limited to pay as you go, as you will not have credit, or need a long contract on the phone. Mobile phones are very popular in the UK, and most students who study there for any length of time will have them. Many retail outlets sell these, so shop around for the best price.
Credit/Debit Cards	If you are planning on using either of these types of cards in the UK, make sure that you have signed the back of them. The cashier will take the card and hold it until you have signed the receipt and will verify that the signatures match.

Eating in a Pub	Most pubs serve food for lunch and in the afternoon. Some do serve food later, but these will be fewer and harder to find. To order food in pubs, choose a table, the menus will be there, and then order at the bar, telling the cashier which table to bring the food.
Eating at Restaurants	Restaurant experiences are often longer and more expensive than those in the US, as eating out is generally a more social occasion and people do this less in the UK. Don't be surprised if the service is slow and the experience takes a couple of hours. Many people will go to drink and eat and have a leisurely time. You will also find that many restaurants are not child friendly in the UK.
Emergency Calls	The emergency dialing code in the UK is 999 or 112. This is what you need to be connected to the police, ambulance, or fire services. The operator will confirm the number you are calling from and your location. These calls are free from any phone.
Free Refills	Most restaurants will not give free refill on soft drinks, or any other drinks besides water, so don't expect it unless it is specifically stated on the menu. The cost you see for a soft drink is the cost of one only, ordering another one will be charged at the same amount.

Floors	In Europe the lowest floor, which is the first floor in the US, is called the ground floor. The first floor up is the first floor in the UK, or sometimes called the "one up". This means that all floors will be numbered differently than you are used to in the US.
Local Calls	You will pay to make any phone call in the UK unless it is a free phone number (starting 0800). This includes local calls and is one more reason to get a local phone card. You will need it to make all phone calls, even local ones.
Gas/Petrol	When buying gasoline for cars, you may think that the price is inexpensive. Remember that the prices on the signs are per liter and there are about four liters in a US gallon. Most of the time, gas (or petrol as it is called in the UK) is between $4 and $6 a gallon.
Groceries	When you check out at the grocery store, you will be required to sack your own items. You will need to do this as they are being totaled at the check out so that the flow of traffic remains smooth. Do not wait in expectation of someone coming to help; this will be your responsibility. The grocery store will supply bags for the groceries, but they do sometimes charge for them.
Normal Business Hours	Most people work from 9am or 9:30 am until 5pm or 5:30pm. Do not expect businesses to be open before this with the exception of doctors' offices.

Off License	To buy alcohol in the UK, other than at the supermarket, you will need to go to an "Off License". These specialty shops sell alcoholic beverages and some small items like sodas and snacks. These stores are open later than grocery stores, until 10 or 11pm generally.
Paying on Buses	If you board a bus at the front door by the driver, you must pay him or her or show your pass. If you board at the rear of the bus then move quickly to your seat. A ticket collector will come to you and check your ticket or sell you one. Do not block the flow of traffic if you are getting on this type of bus. Move quickly to your seat.
Pay Phones	If you need to make a call on a pay phone you must first deposit 20 pence. The phone will then count down the amount of money left and cut you off when the money runs out. This is a straight forward system as you will always know how much credit you have and can add more change as you talk. You pay per minute for all calls including local ones.
Sales Tax	When you buy an item in the UK you will pay the price it is marked, rather than adding sales tax at the register. This will mean that if you pick up an item for £10, you only pay £10 at the cash register. You are paying 17.5% VAT on most items, but this has already been added to the price. You may be eligible for a VAT refund when you return to the US. You can check these rules in the airport when you arrive or return. To receive the VAT refund you must have all receipts with you.

[handwritten note: have you heard about a refund?]

Shopping

You may regularly shop at small corner markets or even small chain supermarkets. Many larger shopping centers and larger grocery stores are outside of the city center shopping. In the city you may have to buy at many different stores, rather than one super center that carries all types of products. You may buy a few products from the drug store, other goods from the grocery store, yet other items from the paper store. Super center type shopping facilities are generally outside of cities.

Store Opening Hours

Most grocery stores are open until 9pm or 10pm, and a few are open 24 hours. This will vary by the size of the city in which you live. Non-grocery stores on the High Street, which is the name of the local street with the majority of shops, will generally close around 6pm. There are late night shopping hours at some stores, on Wednesday or Thursday evenings. On these nights stores may remain open until 8pm or 9pm. In out-of-town shopping centers, stores will generally be open longer.

Taxis

Black cabs are the official taxis in London. In London you can use private companies that use private cars to drive and are called mini cabs. While the mini cabs may be cheaper, it is generally safer to use a black cab, especially at night or if you are new to a city or environment. You can either get a cab by standing in line at a taxi rank, which will be clearly marked, or hailing one on the street if the orange light is illuminated. Mini-cabs do not have meters and it is best to agree a price before you leave.

Television	If you buy or rent a television, you will need to get a TV license. This is a tax that allows for the state owned television stations to be funded. This is why the British Broadcasting Corporations (BBC) channels do not have commercials. Television shows may only be 20 minutes long, especially if they have been bought from the US market, so not all shows run on the hour or half an hour.
Tipping	When it comes to tipping in restaurants make sure that service is not included before you leave extra money. If the tip is not included, then a 10% tip is adequate. It is never necessary to tip in a pub.
Time	Most industries in the UK run on the 24 hour clock, so you will not see am or pm after times. To figure the times out just subtract 12 from military time.
Train Tickets	You will need to buy your train ticket before leaving on your journey. Many train stations have barriers through which you must insert the ticket in order to travel. If you arrive at the station and there is no one to buy a ticket from, or the machines do not work, buy a "permit to travel" from the machine. This shows that you made an effort to buy a ticket. If you are unable to buy one, board the train and the ticket collector can sell you one on the journey. If no one collects tickets, you may have to pay for one to pass through the barriers when you leave the station. If you are taking a long train journey, remember to buy a ticket in advance. You can do this on the internet, over the phone,

	or at the train station. You will pay considerably less if you book ahead of time, sometimes as much as two weeks.
Water	When ordering water you will be asked "still" or "sparkling". Still is mineral water in a bottle, sparkling is with gas or bubbles in it. You will be charged for either, so you may want to order tap water instead. Tap water is generally free of charge.
Queuing	In the UK you need to remember that everyone queues, or stands in line. This is a strict custom everywhere from the grocery store to most events. You will find some circumstances where this is less true, on the tube in London for example.

You may find that there are several cashiers open at places but one central line forms and the person at the front will then go to the first available cashier. Other times you will simply find a cashier and wait for your turn. In any case it is considered very bad manners not to queue or to "queue-jump". |

Although no one could make an exhaustive list of cultural nuances that one needs when living abroad, hopefully these are some of the most common and most striking differences. These tips are designed to help you get started; but, I suspect that after your time abroad, you will be able to double this list.

Special Section:
Dr. H's Top UK Tips
(or How NOT to Look Like a Tourist)

1. Crossing the street
Although crossing the street may seem like a pretty straight forward thing to do, please remember that in the UK they not only drive on the other side of the road, but traffic is coming opposite of what you will expect. Most major cities will have painted "look right" or "look left" signs on the curbs, but my advice is to always follow the green man. When you get to a traffic light, simply push the button and wait for the green man to tell you it is safe to cross. Although the British man in front of you may cross on the red, take your time and play it safe. Every year at least one student ends up in the emergency room because of this problem.

2. Wow- everyone keeps giving me the peace sign.
No, that may not be the peace sign. In the UK making a peace sign, but having the back of your hand to someone is a rude gesture. It is only a peace sign where the front of the hand (the side with the palm) is showing. On a similar note, make sure you are not using this misunderstood symbol either. If you are ordering two of something or signaling two to someone, make sure you aren't accidentally telling them something rude! Most people will forgive you for being a tourist, but it is still not polite.

3. The alphabet doesn't end in zed!
In the UK and Europe; the plain old "z" is pronounced zed!

4. Potatoes, potatoes everywhere, but not a vegetable to eat.

Potatoes are the national vegetable of the UK. I can remember sitting down for meals and having mashed potatoes, French fries, and boiled potatoes all on the same plate. You may be surprised to get so many potatoes and in so many forms-mashed, roasted, baked, chips, crisps, and boiled. Even whole meals, like a jacket potato revolve around this starch. With a jacket potato, the potato itself is split and filled with sandwich filling rather than using bread. You will see them stuffed with tuna, cole slaw, cheese, cottage cheese, chili, beans and a variety of other fillings. I recommend them-you will learn to love them because they are everywhere and cheap.

5. Those are white! New tennis shoes: The American tourist identification system.

Yes, it does seem like every tourist gets a new pair of tennis shoes, or "trainers" as they are called in the UK. These are the international symbol for tourist. I do recommend good walking shoes as so much of your time is spent walking, but try to tame the wild colors in your wardrobe. Most people in the UK wear dark colors and seldom wear tennis shoes at all!

[handwritten: Oops →]

6. No, not everyone is an alcoholic.

While it may seem like all activities center around drinking, try to expand your thinking to the fact that most center around the pub rather than alcohol. The pub has been the center of social life in villages and small towns for centuries and remains so today. Pubs are simply where communities are formed and are often meeting places for friends, families, and neighbors. Remember that pubs also serve food (the pub lunch) and you can drink non alcoholic beverages there. Try an orange juice and lemonade if drinking the local ale isn't your style.

7. No need to yell, I can hear you.

While on public transportation and in public places, most people will talk softly or rarely speak to others. This is a huge difference for those from the US who may be used to speaking to everyone and getting a friendly response. This also varies throughout the country. If you are on a train, bus or tube, the only people you will hear speaking are most likely the tourists (you can check this against the color and newness of their tennis shoes). You may also notice that people in the UK are more reserved. You may know someone for some time but know very little about their personal or business life. The self disclosure that Americans are used to is not the norm in other places.

8. Please take a guide book!

If I had 10p for every time someone asked me what and where Big Ben was I would be a rich woman. As with any city you need to take a guide book and quit bothering the locals for tourist information! How many times have you been asked about something in your own town and you have no idea why it is historic? (Get my hint??) When you take a day to sightsee, the best value really is one of those tourist buses or a walking tour. But if you go it alone in the subway, take your guide book and don't rely on others for directions and tourist information. They may simply not know or they may be playing the old "give the tourist the wrong information game".

9. How can anyone NOT love the tube?

Another one of the mysteries of London. I hear people who have toured through London say how much they love the tube, or the subway. When I snicker and say that only tourists love the tube they often look at me as though I am crazy. But, no, I am not crazy - this is true. Most tourists will have day passes or week long passes which are only valid after 9:30am. The rush hour is over by the time they get on the subway and it all seems fine. If you were to travel early, like the millions who live in London, you would find higher prices, long lines, and trains so full that you cannot breathe. Most who live in London agree that they can not live without the tube, but it is also difficult to live with.

10. So, what are these people talking about?

Many tourists think that since we all speak English, there will be no difficulty with communication. This is simply not the case. Just as you use US slang that bears no resemblance to the meaning of the word, the British do to. Add to this local dialect and other oddities such as Cockney rhyming slang it may have you "taking a butchers" at one of those dictionaries explaining the differences between English and American. It may be worth a few quid to pick one up! (See what I mean?)

Chapter 6
Travel in the UK

You will experience two kinds of travel during your stay in the UK, day to day travel on trains, buses, and subways, and traveling for fun. There is a lot you need to know about both types of travel. This chapter offers a basic guide for both types of travel and tips for cheaper tickets, and ideas for great places to visit.

Essential Travel

In your everyday life you may be required to use more public transportation than you have ever used before. While on occasion you may be able to travel in a private car, and your university may provide shuttle services, you will most likely ride a bus, train, or subway (often called the Tube in London). Even if you live in a small town or village you may find the bus service a link to shopping or entertainment. I would encourage you to take advantage of the transportation that your university offers. Many times they will arrange excursions or day trips that are generally less expensive than going alone. While public transportation is not difficult to use, for some it is a new challenge.

Many universities will give you guides for the local area when you arrive. Another great source for information is other students. If you have flat mates or friends who have lived in the area or attended the university for some time, they will be the best starting place for information. You will need to find the best resource for local transportation and remember, this may mean more than one type. I regularly used the trains, buses, and tube in one journey.

Trains

The first consideration is whether or not you can use a youth discount. If you are going to be riding a train very often, or planning to travel throughout the UK, then you may want to invest in a Young Person's Railcard. You can get this if you are 16 to 25 years old or an older full time student. This rail card costs £18 for one year and is good on most trains and some ferry services. Using this card will give you a third off most rail fares and may quickly pay for itself if you use the train often – sometimes in one journey if you are going a longer distance.

The easiest way to find train times is through online sources, such as www.thetrainline.com or Network Rail. You can enter your starting point and your destination and these websites will figure a route and give you train times and prices too in the case of thetrainline.com. You can also look at the train station where they should have monitors showing the train's destination, stops en-route, and whether or not the train has been delayed. Trains do try and keep their schedules so you need to be at the train station on time. Trains are run by a variety of different companies but you can buy a ticket for all companies from your local station. Be aware that you often cannot use your ticket on certain routes which have a variety of operators. If you are riding a long distance, you must take the train operated by the company from whom you bought a ticket.

Buses

Buses are owned and run by many different companies, so it is difficult to predict if they will have a student discount. Ask when you board a bus, but have your student identification card handy and be prepared to pay full price just in case. Most buses will have timetables posted next to bus stops. Keep in mind that buses may not actually run on these schedules, but more on an as they come basis. Some bus stops will have monitors that tell when the buses will arrive. Not all buses stop at all stops. You must be aware of whether you are at the correct stop. If it is a request stop, you must hail the bus by waving.

Long distance buses (or coaches) are operated mainly by National Express. Again, they offer a student discount card and are generally cheaper (and slower) than the trains. Some routes do have other operators, such as the popular London to Oxford routes.

Subway

Probably the most famous subway system in the UK is the tube in London. Even if you are only visiting London you will use this as your major form of transport. Glasgow has an underground as well, which goes in a circle through the city, so you really can't go wrong.

To get a student discount on the tube in London you will need to obtain a photocard though the student's union at your university or pick up a form at a tube station. This is only for 7 day pass or you can buy longer season tickets that are valid on the buses and tubes. No student discounts for daily travel cards or single tickets are available. Transportation systems in cities outside of London may also require a photo card and you should ask before buying your ticket if a student discount exists.

Many times you can buy a day pass or weekend pass that will allow you to use all the different forms of transportation in a city for an allotted amount of time. If you use public transportation every day, you may also want to invest in a weekly or monthly pass. You do save money with these passes, especially if you expect to travel a lot. You will need a photo with you to purchase these at underground stations or some authorized dealers such as small corner shops. Most places that sell these cards will display notices in their windows.

Subway schedules are printed and posted at most stations, but these too are not strictly adhered to except for the first and last trains of the day. Some underground stations will have electronic boards that keep the schedules and next train arrival information. While knowing when the train will arrive is one important issue, perhaps the most important thing to know is when the last train, bus or tube will run. Once the public transportation system has stopped running you may find yourself facing a lengthy walk or taking a taxi. In some places taxi fares go up at night, so be sure to know your schedule.

Taxis

Unless you live in a big city, taking taxis may be a new experience for you. As you will soon realize, buses, trains, and subways will get you close to some places but not exactly all the way there. Public transport also stops running at some point, so you may have to take a taxi or a night bus to get home. You will take a black cab, except in London where you may also take a mini cab. You can hail a black cab or wait for one at a taxi rank, but remember that the later it is the more difficult it will be to get transportation. Taxis will be more expensive, so if you can share them it will be more economical. Also, if you are in London all of the black taxi drivers must have passed a test called "the knowledge"; that demonstrates their knowledge of the city. So they should know how to get where you want to go without too much explaining. Always give the street address and perhaps a landmark that your destination is close to, but you will find that most taxi drivers will know how to get there better than you do.

Always leave yourself time for any problems that may arise with public transportation. Unseen problems can make you late. If you have an important meeting or exam, leave earlier than usual to avoid any of these problems. If there are severe problems with public transportation, ask the information staff if an alternate route exists. There are generally other ways to get where you are going, but this may also take some time and be less direct to your location.

Sightseeing in the UK

When making your travel plans in the UK, I suggest buying a travel guide that will give you specific information about the locations, accommodations, places to eat, and the most important sights to see. When planning your travels through the country, you can use chapter 11 to map out your journeys. Remember that you may find as much beauty and history in the small towns and villages as in the larger cities. You may want to make a combination of two when planning your journey.

In making your plans to travel in the UK, remember to reserve train tickets early. Most of the inexpensive tickets must be purchased one to two weeks in advance. You may also find that flying on some of the budget airlines will be less expensive and much quicker than the train. You may also want to plan your time to see two or more places that are along the same route, thus saving money on travel expenses.

Below is a list of larger and smaller cities that you may want to consider putting on your itinerary. I have also suggested historical sights, castles, and other places that students typically like to see. You can use these suggestions, along with your travel guide, to make plans. This is in no way a complete list, as you may find some hidden places or small villages that are worthy of a visit. Keep them in your diary to recommend to others.

England	
Bath	An original Roman town where you can still visit the Roman Baths and other attractions. Bath has a lot of lovely things to see and is in beautiful countryside too. Don't forget the American Museum housed just outside of Bath which has several original houses and artifacts from "the colonies" that became the United States.
Birmingham	Birmingham is the second largest city in the UK. The centre of the city is in the middle of a large redevelopment plan, with the town hall and convention centre already complete.
Bournemouth	A beach town that may be best known for its retirement communities. If you are hoping to walk along the beaches and take in some sea air, this is a good place to do so.
Brighton	On the coast, this city has a pier and boasts the Royal Pavilion. You can walk along the beach, shop the lanes, or stay later for the nightlife.
Cambridge	Choose a nice day to visit and go punting at Cambridge. A beautiful university and town to shop for the mandatory t-shirt.

Cotswold's	A range of hills to the west and north west of London. Famous for its small towns and villages constructed from the honey colored Cotswold stone nestled in the hills; this is the place to see the typical English village.
Durham	Visit this medieval city and see the beautiful university, the Durham Dales, the botanic gardens, and take a boat ride on the River Wear.
The Lake District	A beautiful area in the north of England that features lovely small towns, inns, and pubs. A historic and quaint district that holds the charm that you think of when you think of England.
Liverpool	Birthplace of the Beatles. A former port on the west coast, Liverpool has recently been awarded title of European City of Culture for the year 2008.
Leeds	Sitting on the edge of the beautiful Yorkshire Dales, a good place to start exploring this area of England with good transport links to other areas in the north. A large student population gives the town a good nightlife.
London	The capital of England and perhaps one of the most famous cities in the world. You will need a guide to this city alone. You can shop, eat at amazing restaurants, go to the theatre, go clubbing,

	dancing, or on an all night pub crawl. A "must see" if you are in the UK.
Manchester	Hosted the Commonwealth Games in 2002 and as a result of that and an IRA bomb blast a few years earlier the city has undergone considerable redevelopment. It has a vibrant nightlife and has been the home to a number of popular bands. Like many places in the UK, it has a very culturally diverse population.
Newcastle	Perhaps best known for the drink, the largest city in the northeast of England. When there you can visit the university, the museum of antiquities, the castle, cathedral, old city wall, and the river Tyne.
Oxford	Visit some of the colleges and buy a t-shirt or sweatshirt to take home. A nice day out to visit the museums, the university, and shopping in the city.
Salisbury/ Stonehenge	Although you can no longer walk up to the stones, but only on a path set out around them, it remains a "must see" for many. On the journey stop to see Salisbury Cathedral, an extra bonus on this trip – once the tallest building in the world.
Stratford Upon Avon	Great shopping and a must for Shakespeare fans. You can plan a whole day around these attractions

	to visit all of the places that he and his family lived in.
Winchester	Once the capital of Wessex - an area in the south of England from where King Alfred the Great ruled. Today the city is a small market town with a range of shops and restaurants, and its medieval cathedral.
York	Only a few hours by train from London and a good day out. It boasts a number of excellent museums ranging from the Jorvik Viking Museum to the National Railways Museum and a museum about life in Britain over the ages. The beautiful Minster and the Mumbles, the medieval shops, and medieval houses are not to be missed.

England Castles and Historic Sights	
Corfe Castle/ The Dorset Coast	On the southern coast are a number of seaside resorts. Corfe Castle is near Swanage and has several things to offer plus beautiful views and unique small villages on the coast. If you enjoy walking, it is a good place to visit staying in bed and breakfasts along your coastal route.
Dover Castle	Although the castle itself has suffered from war and the environment, the real attraction are

	the hidden tunnels in the white cliffs. See how England managed World War II from this vantage point, complete with a tour of the hospital built into these tunnels.
Hadrian's Wall	A Roman wall from AD 122 that still stands in northern England. An impressive sight considering its age and history.
Leeds Castle	Beautiful grounds and a well maintained castle. Go on a nice spring day and take a picnic. Special events are often organized at weekends.
Warwick Castle	A wonderfully kept castle that hosts wax figures showing how the original castle may have been used. Many weekend exhibits also provide great entertainment.
Windsor Castle	A great day trip from London and easily accessible by train. The castle is only one attraction in Windsor. Visit the castle, shop and then visit Eton to see where Princes William and Harry were educated.

Scotland	
Edinburgh	Great city to visit and loved by all. There is a castle, the Royal Mile, and great shopping. Very easy to navigate. Definitely worth the visit and can easily be combined with other Scottish destinations.

Glasgow	Known as more of an industrial city, but a delightful place to visit full of museums and shopping. Many sights make this destination worthwhile and can be easily linked to a trip to Edinburgh. Easy subway system to get around town.
Inverness/ Loch Ness	Go north and look for Nessie. You can easily take a bus trip to Loch Ness from Inverness and catch a boat ride across the Loch. Many people feel this is a must when in Scotland.
Isle of Skye	Go further north and you will see amazing beauty.
St Andrews	The home of golf and Prince William's university. Worth a visit to say you have been.
Sterling/ Sterling Castle	With Braveheart's historical presence, this small town boasts some shopping, a university, a castle and monument to William Wallace.

Wales and Northern Ireland	
Belfast	Some feel that Northern Ireland is too dangerous to visit but the situation is rapidly changing. If you are not interested in visiting Northern Ireland, see the following chapter for information on visiting other places Ireland.

Cardiff	The capital of Wales and a destination for many. You can see many museums and castles while there.
Snowdonia National Park	A place of beauty on this often snow covered peak.

    Some of the places that you see and locations where trips are scheduled will be dictated by the location where you are studying. The university will typically offer day trips, so the location must be relatively close. If you plan to travel to many places in the UK, you should consider a Britrail Pass. These passes allow you to buy a certain number of journeys within a specified period for one price. This is also paid in advance, so you will not have to book tickets along the way or try to economize on the travel. Britrail passes are different from Eurail Passes, as you need a Britrail pass in the UK and Eurail passes in the rest of mainland Europe. These passes are generally less expensive to buy before you come to the UK, rather than while you are there. So they are great going away gifts from friends and family and will allow you to make the most of your time. Remember that a lot of these destinations may be near by, so you can travel on your days away from classes or at weekends, and then plan more time for your trips out of the UK.

Chapter 7
Travel in Europe

One of the main things students are interested in is traveling while studying. This chapter will address how to travel inexpensively and where you may want to go. We will look at ways of travel abroad, such as flying, trains, taking the Eurostar, ferries, and how to book these for as little as possible. Whether you are taking a weekend or a month long trip through Europe this chapter has suggestions for places to visit. Perhaps the most important part of this chapter is the travel cost worksheet, which will help you calculate the total cost of your trips, including the hidden expenses that are easily forgotten. Make copies of this sheet and use it when planning your journeys. It will help to keep you on budget and to make the best plans possible.
Airfare
You may find traveling throughout Europe and even further abroad to be more affordable than you think. With the surge of budget, no frills airlines, there are consistently good bargains. On some flights you may only be required to pay the taxes, making them extremely good value. The downside to these budget airlines is that they generally depart from smaller airports that may be a considerable distance from a city or town, and they also arrive in small airports that

can take some time to travel to and from. You need to consider this when thinking about this bargain because the travel on buses, rail, or tube to get to the airport and your destination once you have arrived may double the prices of these tickets. You also need to consider that the best values will be at odd times, such as early in the morning or late at night, when it may be difficult to get public transportation, and during the middle of the week flights will be less expensive.

You will generally buy two one way tickets on the budget airlines, and you can try many different dates and times to find the best values. These airlines usually do not have assigned seating, but rather you find a seat once aboard. You will also not be given any food or drinks, but you will have the opportunity to buy them on the plane. Once aboard they are considerably more expensive, so you may want to bring something with you or eat beforehand.

Budget carriers are listed below, but remember you may also get student fares that are competitive and with more flexible ticketing options. Try all of these alternatives before making any reservations. Use the worksheet to find which ticket is actually a bargain. I have not listed routes or destinations, as these airlines seem to change quite often. Look at them on line and check for the latest information. The web sites are listed in the appendix.

- Ryanair
- EasyJet
- BMI Baby
- Virgin Express

Budget airlines are worth investigating, but remember that some of the larger carriers have lowered prices to compete and the airports that they fly to and from may be much easier to access. Calculate all of these components when determining the actual price of travel. I have included a worksheet to help with this.

Ferries

The least expensive way to travel on a ferry is as a foot passenger. You board the ferry while the cars are being loaded below. Most ferries have shopping, entertainment, movies and discos on overnight journeys. You can economize on overnight journeys by sleeping in a rest area that generally has seats that look like those found on an airline. You can also book a cabin, although this is more expensive. Cabins generally have two single beds and a small bathroom.

Although ferries will take longer than air or train, they are often very inexpensive for foot passengers and are a unique way to travel. The most common ferry destinations are to France, but you can take them to Germany, Denmark, the Netherlands and beyond. Some ferries take only a couple of hours and others take overnight trips. You will have to get to the coast to get to a ferry port, so there will be an additional expense for the train or bus fare to get to your destination. Once abroad you may also need to take a train or bus to continue on your adventure.

Eurail Pass

Many students who want to take one trip through Europe during one of the longer breaks will purchase a Eurail pass. With this pass you can use the train service in up to 17 countries, including Sweden, Norway, Finland, Ireland, Switzerland, France, Germany, Belgium, the Netherlands, Spain, Portugal, Austria, Greece, Hungary and Denmark. You should check the Eurail website for an up-to-date list of countries and networks where you can use the Eurail pass as the list is constantly changing. (Be aware that you cannot use the Eurail pass in the UK. In the UK you will need a Britrail pass.) There is a variation on the Eurail pass called Eurail-ticket which is valid in more countries but is less flexible.

Many different types of passes are available, from passes that allow different classes of travel, different counties and shipping networks. But the main difference is the amount that you are allowed to travel over a specified time. Some passes allow for ten to fifteen days of travel within a two month period, while some allow for consecutive travel within a specified period of two weeks to many months. You will need to choose the pass that is right for your time and journey plans. The wonderful thing about buying these passes is the freedom that they allow. You can change plans or stay in a place longer or shorter than you originally had projected. Many students find this freedom to be the best way to travel, so that as you see new places you can change plans on the way.

Remember to buy your Eurail pass before you leave for study abroad. Your days for travel do not start until the pass is validated on the first train. For a discount, those coming from the US can buy them before they arrive in Europe. Please see appendix B for suggestions on where to buy them.

Hostels

Without a doubt the least expensive places to stay while traveling are hostels. Youth hostels are available all over the world and offer good services at a lower standard than a hotel. Most offer dorm type accommodations with shared bathrooms and some cooking facilities. Hostels will vary greatly between the type of accommodations and their appearances. Some will be in beautiful locations and have immaculate bedrooms and bathrooms. Others will be of a lower standard. In many hostels you have the opportunity to choose the accommodation that is right for you. The least expensive is generally a dorm type room where you will have a bunk bed and access to shared restrooms. Some hostels offer private and semi private rooms for a larger fee, so you can upgrade if you wish to. Always remember to bring a few items with you if you are staying in a hostel, like a towel and your toiletries. These will not be provided for you. Most hostels will have lockers for you to leave belongings while you are out. The best way to find out about a particular hostel is to access online resources. You can also get information and reviews from others who have traveled to places you are interested in.

Hostels are set up for travelers who are on a budget. They allow you to cook some of your own food rather than always eating out. They also put you in touch with others who are traveling and allow the chance to meet other people and make friends. The staff is a great source of information as they deal with this type of clientele all of the time.

You may find that when you travel as a group you can use a less expensive hotel for the same price as a hostel. Some hotels will accommodate three or four individuals in one room. Sometimes hostels are better located than less expensive hotels, so keep in mind the cost of travel to the sights and getting home in the evenings. You will also have to eat outside of your hotel and this may add to the costs of travel as well. I always recommend going to the supermarket and using the hotel mini bar to refrigerate your items if possible. This may not always be possible, especially in some economy hotels.

Eurostar

A great way to travel to France or Belgium is on the Eurostar, the passenger train that leaves from London and goes directly to Paris, Brussels, and other locations, such as Disneyland Paris and some ski resorts depending on the season. The Eurostar is a passenger train that takes two to three hours to reach its destination. You travel above ground until you reach the English Channel, where you cross under the channel. This transit only takes twenty to thirty minutes and then you return to above ground train travel when you emerge in France. The Eurostar has a dining car, but one should consider taking your own snacks as the dining car is expensive and serves fast food.

Student fares are available on this service and some day trip fares are very competitive. You can buy a student flexipass before you leave the US and use this as an open departure once in the UK. Again, once you reach the terminus, you will need to take public transportation to the sights but it is not as far (or expensive) as having to travel from the airport. You may also need to add train tickets or flights to London if you are living outside of the city. If you are close to or studying in London, the Eurostar provides a great opportunity. You can start your journey in Europe this way or take a short trip. The great part is that once in London you can take the tube to the train. You may find it faster to take the Eurostar than flying as the train stops in the center of Paris and the check-in times for the train are less extensive than at the airport.

Remember to buy your ticket beforehand, book early, and leave yourself plenty of time to arrive and check in. It may take some adjustment to find your way through the train stations once you arrive on the continent. Take a guide book or city map so that you can find your way to the city center and the sights you are most interested in.

Places to Go

There are so many places that you may consider traveling to while you are abroad that one book could never cover all of them. I have listed a group of capital cities that are popular with students and places that many people visit. This in no way should limit your thinking about where to go and what type of adventure to have. You may find that by going on budget airlines you can travel to smaller cities that are less well known but are still amazing places to see. You may also find that your travel itinerary is dependent on others, so these major cities may never feature in your trips. In any case, I have made some suggestions for countries and cities to visit. When you do decide where you will travel, research these destinations more fully, buy a guide book or map, or search the internet for more information.

France - Paris

Paris is one of the most beautiful cities in the world. France is both easily accessible from the UK and is a very common destination. If you are traveling from London to Paris, consider the Eurostar. If you plan to make your way through France, you may want to consider a ferry crossing. You can cross to Calais from Dover or to many ports in Normandy from the south coast of England.

In France you may want to consider visiting small villages, the World War II monuments and beaches, the castles and chateaux of the Loire Valley, the beaches and resorts, or the capital city of Paris. No matter where you plan to travel in France, you can expect good food, beautiful scenery, and amazing history.

If you are visiting Paris, there are countless museums and attractions to visit. You can navigate through the city easily on the subway, or metro as it is called, which is very straightforward to use. Make sure to plan your visit, as it would take weeks to see everything and you may have to choose between several places. Consider visiting the Eiffel Tower, Cathedral of Notre Dame, the Louvre, the Champs Elysée, and the Arc de Triomphe. These are just a few of the amazing sights to consider.

Belgium - Brussels, Bruges

Belgium is another country that is very easy to travel to via coach and ferry, flight, or Eurostar. I recommend Brussels or Bruges, but again you may find other places to see. Both of these cities are beautiful with a lot to see and can be navigated each in a day or two. The other advantage that many find here is that almost everyone will speak English and you will have no difficulty with communicating.

Brussels is the capital of Belgium and a wonderful place to visit, buy souvenirs of tapestries, lace, and of course - chocolate. The main square is full of restaurants and cafes with outside seating perfect for a meal in the sunshine and to relax before taking in the sights. You can easily walk to most of the sights from the main square, so all you need is a map of the area from the tourist information office. You may also want a guide book to help you find the best places to visit. In the evening why not have some mussels in Brussels on the main dining street? This is a narrow street packed with restaurants, outside seating, and lively commentary from the waiters.

Bruges is a smaller city and an ancient city built with a canal system that you can tour. The boat tour is a highlight of the city, along with the main square, small quaint restaurants, and shopping for all your Belgium items and more chocolate. Although Bruges is not a capital city, the architecture and friendliness of this small town will bring you back again and again.

Netherlands - Amsterdam

    Almost every student has Amsterdam on their list of places to see. Amsterdam is accessible by ferry, flight, or train with many connections throughout Europe if you are traveling on a Eurail pass. The city boasts everything from culture to nightlife. Most people love the contrast between places like the Van Gogh Museum and Ann Frank's house while still being able to party at the variety of discos and clubs. Amsterdam is also an unusual sight for many who are used to the more restrictive attitudes of the United States. Don't be surprised by the liberal attitudes towards sex and drugs in this capital city, take it as a cultural experience and to distinguish how attitudes about certain issues can differ from country to country.

Spain - Madrid and Ibiza

    Another top spot for visiting is Spain. You can catch up on the sunshine while you take in all that this country has to offer. There are many wonderful places to visit here that I cannot include them all in this section, but remember that you may want to go further a field and visit cities like Barcelona. Make your plans with your guide book and consider all of your options, I don't think you can go wrong when choosing a destination in Spain.

    Madrid is the capital city and a popular place to visit. You can spend your days in art museums like the Prado, visiting the historic plazas, or the many cafes and restaurants that the city has to offer. There are numerous sightseeing options in Madrid and just outside, all accessible by the subway or train system. Spain is known for its nightlife and its famous siestas. Remember that most of the shops will close in the afternoons and reopen for late hours in the evenings, when most of the population will come out for the vibrant nightlife.

    Ibiza is another common place for students to visit. An island off the coast of Spain, it is known for its outrageous hedonism. If you want to holiday in a place that is all sun and nightlife, then Ibiza may be your destination. Countless bars, clubs, and discos keep the nightlife going from sunset to sunrise.

Italy - Rome, Pisa, Venice

    Many students put Italy in the list of places to visit. It is a diverse country that has many well known landmarks, amazing cities, and of course great food. I have suggested just three cities that you may want to consider when planning your trips. Some people go to Italy and travel for many weeks to see the diversity between the north and the south, as well as a taste of all of the regional specialties.

Rome is the capital city and has many of the famous monuments such as the Coliseum, Trevi Fountain and Spanish Steps. Many also visit the Vatican while in Rome to see the Sistine Chapel and St Paul's Cathedral. Pisa is best known for the Leaning Tower and Venice for its canals. No matter which city you decide to visit, you will enjoy all of the art, architecture, and pasta that one can indulge in.

Ireland - Dublin

Ireland is a wonderful contrast to the United Kingdom. It is a country that may look as though it belongs with the UK but is different in almost every way. Ireland is known for its lush green landscapes, its friendly people, and of course, Guinness. When you visit Dublin, accessible by ferry, train and ferry, or air, you can visit the Guinness factory and have a sample of this dark ale. You can also visit the many museums, universities, and pubs that the city offers. Dublin is a great weekend away and an easy destination to get to. I would highly recommend it for your list of places to visit.

Whichever destination you chose, remember that your time abroad is one of the best opportunities you will ever have to travel. The UK is well located to other destinations, and travel from the UK is a fraction of what the trips would cost from the US. Take advantage of this and see as much as you can. But, be mindful that you are there to study abroad, so don't miss too many classes or let grades slip while you are off in a foreign port.

Travel cost work sheet
SAMPLE

Trip from __London_____ to _____Paris_____

Getting there
Flight Details:
Carrier__**Eurostar**_____
Departure flight date: _____**10/13/04**_____
Departure flight time: _____**9:50am**_____
Departure flight number: _____**Train 76**__
Departure flight cost: _____**$70**_____

Airport Details: How will I get from my university/ flat to the departure airport? Travel Details (train, bus, tube): ____
I will take the tube from my flat to London Waterloo

Cost of travel to airport: __**$5**_____

Arrival Details
What airport will I arrive at?
_____**Paris Gare du Nord**_____

How far is this from the place you are visiting?
_**I want to visit Paris city center, so this is about 15 minutes away**

How will I travel from this airport to the city/ sights?
_____**Metro**_____

Times that this transportation runs:
_____**all day**_____
_____
_____

Cost for this transportation: _____**$7 day pass**_____

Accommodation Details
Where will I stay? ___**Paris Hostel**_____

Cost Per Night? _____**$25**_____

Other Expenses
Estimated Cost for food:
_____**$20 a day for 3 days =$60**_____

Sightseeing/ Entrance fees: _____**$50**_____

Daily Travel Budget (train, bus, underground passes)
_____**$7 per day for metro pass**_____

Return Flight Details
   Carrier_____**Eurostar**_____
   Return flight date: _____**10/16/04**_____
   Return flight time: ____**7pm**_____
   Return flight number: ___**Train 78**_____
   Return flight cost: _____**$70**_____

Airport Details: How will I get from my hotel/ hostel to the airport?
Travel Details (train, bus, tube):
_____**I will take the metro**_____
_____
_____

Cost of travel to airport:
_____**Already have day pass**_____

Arrival Details
What airport will I arrive at?
_____**London Waterloo**_____

How far is this from the place your university/ flat?
_____**15 minutes**_____

How will I travel from this airport to my university/ flat?
_____**London underground**_____

Times that this transportation runs:
_____**until 12am**_____

Cost of this transportation to your university/ flat: ___**$5**_____

Total Cost of travel for this trip:
Airfare	_$140_
Travel to airport from university/ flat	_$5__
Travel to hotel/ hostel upon arrival	_$7__
Accommodation Expense	_$75_
Sightseeing Expenses	_$50_
Food Budget	_$60_
Transportation Budget	_$14_
Travel from hotel/ hostel to airport	__x__
Travel from airport to University/ flat	_$5__
Other:	
TOTAL	_$356_

Travel cost work sheet

Trip from _____ to _____

Getting There
Flight Details:
        Carrier_____
        Departure flight date: _____
        Departure flight time: _____
        Departure flight number: _____
        Departure flight cost: _____

Airport Details: How will I get from my university/ flat to the departure airport?
Travel Details (train, bus, tube):
_____
_____
_____
_____

Cost of travel to airport: _____

Arrival Details
What airport will I arrive at? _____

How far is this from the place you are visiting?
_____
_____
_____

How will I travel from this airport to the city/ sights?
_____
_____
_____
_____
_____

Times that this transportation runs:
_____
_____
_____

Cost for this transportation: _____

Accommodation Details
Where will I stay? _____
Cost Per Night? _____

Other Expenses
Estimated Cost for food: _____
Sightseeing/ Entrance fees: _____
Daily Travel Budget (train, bus, underground passes)
_____

Return Flight Details
        Carrier_____
        Return flight date: _____
        Return flight time: _____
        Return flight number: _____
        Return flight cost: _____

Airport Details: How will I get from my hotel/ hostel to the airport?
Travel Details (train, bus, tube):
_____
_____
_____
_____

Cost of travel to airport: _____

Arrival Details
What airport will I arrive at? _____

How far is this from the place your university/ flat?
_____
_____
_____

How will I travel from this airport to my university/ flat?
_____
_____
_____

Times that this transportation runs:
_____
_____
_____

Cost of this transportation to your university/ flat: _____

Total Cost of travel for this trip:
    Airfare _____
    Travel to airport from university/ flat _____
    Travel to hotel/ hostel upon arrival _____
    Accommodation Expense _____
    Sightseeing Expenses _____
    Food Budget _____
    Transportation Budget _____
    Travel from hotel/ hostel to airport _____
    Travel from airport to University/ flat _____
    Other: _____

    TOTAL _____

Chapter 8
Advice from the Experts

I have asked students from all over the world five questions about their experiences, from pre-departure through their time abroad. Here you can get advice from others who have been in the same, or similar, circumstances, but also give you reassurance for the difficult times ahead. Everyone finds different things about study abroad rewarding or frustrating, so here are some specifics that may help you. Remember that in any circumstance you are not alone; others have had similar feelings and experiences. Reading these may make you excited about leaving for your adventure or may help you through tough times. I hope that the many viewpoints expressed here will give you valuable information.

What do you wish that you had been told before leaving to study abroad?

"I wish I had been more in touch with the school that I was going to before I actually got there. I would have liked to have known how big my room was and what the campus had to offer as far as rental items. I brought sheets and blankets

and found out once I got there that they just took up space in my suitcase because they provided all of that for me at school."
Laurel, 22, North Carolina

"I wish I had been better informed about the costs of studying abroad, in particular London. I quickly managed to find employment, but as anywhere, money was always tight."
Jeroen, 21, the Netherlands

"I believe that no matter what people say to you before you leave, it just sounds like lecturing, preaching. You only have to explore the reality of it yourself to understand that you can win, you can be strong."
Anastasia, 20, Russia

"One can be told many things, pieces of advice from people trying to be helpful, but many of these pieces got lost in the jumble of counsel. I wish that I had been told clearly and directly how best to contact friends and family at home in the States. Of course there is the traditional e-mailing, and telephoning, but HOW to do this in another country is baffling and frustrating even when the language is your own. Telephone exchange numbers are obviously different, but are easy enough to "decode". However I had stocked up on American calling cards, to only find out that their connecting power was moot. Another little tidbit or rather, another rather large tidbit is money. *You can never have too much money.* There are many more discounts for students than for regular citizens, especially in Europe. However there is so much to do and see that many sacrifices will need to be made in the name of fun and/or travel. Get a credit card and max it out if you have to. Coming home to bills is no fun, but being debt free with the 'I should have' cloud over your head is worse."
Mary Kate, 23, Massachusetts

"I wish that someone would have told me to study abroad for an entire year instead of only a semester because it would have saved me a lot of paperwork and headaches when I decided to stay for an extra semester. There is so much available to study

abroad students and a semester just isn't enough time to experience it all."
Christy, 20, North Carolina

"Before leaving for study abroad, I wish I had been told to pack as lightly as possible. There is always that tendency to try and pack every possible thing that you feel that you are going to need. In reality most students will only use about half what they feel they will need."
Jeff, 20, North Carolina

What has been the most frustrating thing about studying abroad?

"In the beginning, it was the adjustment period. It is a very frustrating time when your body and mind adjusts to different things around you. In my case, if found the accents of the people around me difficult to understand. The English grading system was also difficult to adjust to and frustrating when first introduced – I didn't understand why I could not get 100% on an assignment."
Nick, 20, Ohio

"The most frustrating thing about studying abroad was trying to accommodate people who wanted to come visit me. I loved having my friends and family come over, but I felt like I was spending too much time to tour guide them around all the cool places I had found and not enough time trying to check out new places. I also missed out on some school activities that I would have loved to join in on so that my friends could come visit. Like I said, I loved having them there, but being expected to make accommodations when I was trying to navigate my own way around the city got a little frustrating!"
Laurel, 22, North Carolina

"The most frustrating thing about studying abroad has probably been the lack of understanding for the culture I find myself in. Coming from the continent, it was quite a culture shock arriving in England. Having lived in 7 countries in 18 years has helped a great deal with adjusting though. Generally

the atmosphere at university was very welcoming, and I experienced little trouble fitting in as a foreigner. This however was not the case in places of work, which surprised me."
Jeroen, 21, the Netherlands

"It was very difficult to open a bank account because the restrictions in England are very strange."
Bastian, 23, Germany

"Differences in culture, peoples' behavior, attitudes, lifestyle. Getting used to all of this. Feeling lonely. Sometimes prejudice against nationality, rarely though."
Anastasia, 20, Russia

"When I first returned to the US, I would have said that leaving, or not knowing when I would be returning London, was the most frustrating. I still have yet to return, I think I will have to still say that not yet making it back is the most frustrating. It's funny that over time I can really only remember all the good times I had and nothing bad at all."
Mary Kate, 23, Massachusetts

"The most frustrating part about studying abroad is the fact that transportation is sometimes a problem. While living in London, I felt like I wasn't able to do as much as I would have liked to because I had to work around someone else's schedule instead of my own."
Jeff, 20, North Carolina

"For me, the most frustrating thing about studying abroad was the paperwork and communication issues between my home university and host university. The different time zones made communicating difficult and the paperwork seemed endless. In the end, it was totally worth it! "
Christy, 20, North Carolina

What is the best thing about studying abroad?

"People are the best thing about studying abroad. Meeting people from all around the world creates an awareness and appreciation of the world that you may never understand until you indulge yourself in that lifestyle. Meeting people from countries around the world is certainly the best thing about studying abroad."
Nick, 20, Ohio

"The best thing about studying abroad was meeting all the different people. I left the States thinking I would keep myself away from Americans for five months no matter what it took. Once I got there, I realized that Americans were great to hook up with because they wanted to travel and try all the new things I wanted to try. It was also great getting to know the locals, because they were more than willing to take you home for a weekend. You got to see different parts of the country and get a feel for what real life is like there. Getting involved in international organizations and activities was also great because you met people from everywhere!"
Laurel, 22, North Carolina

"The best thing about studying abroad has been getting acquainted with new cultures. I really liked embracing the British culture while at the same time getting to know many other people from places I had never heard of. This has been a great experience."
Jeroen, 21, the Netherlands

"I really enjoy being with English and International students at university. Another fact is that many people want to meet you as a person because they are interested in your country. You also have sometimes a kind of special role, because you are international and everybody accepts that you sometimes might not have the knowledge of the language in the country you are studying in. Study abroad helps to improve your international experience and, of course, your language skills."
Bastian, 23, Germany

"Meeting new, interesting people: from all over the world is definitely one of the strongest advantages and pleasures you might say. Getting to explore the different culture, different languages, and different lifestyle plus the ability to travel. And also, when you study abroad it makes you realize how precious your own country is. How dear and important all of your family and friends are to you. You get to appreciate them more!"
Anastasia, 20, Russia

"This is the easiest question to answer because even when things didn't go as planned, they went right. The single best thing I took from this experience is the friendships I made with both my American companions and foreign students I lived and learned with. It's always fun to gather with your American friends when you get home to reminisce about all the adventures and crazy nights. However it's extra exciting to meet up with international friends whether at your home or if lucky enough, at theirs. It gives you great places to visit."
Mary Kate, 23, Massachusetts

"The best thing about studying abroad is the traveling experience itself. Especially if studying in Europe or the UK, the opportunities to travel are endless. Travel seems much cheaper there and flying or taking the train should be a very frequent occurrence so students are able to see every thing possible in the short amount of time they will be there."
Jeff, 20, North Carolina

"The best thing about studying abroad was challenging myself to leave the comforts of friends, family, and everything that was familiar to me, and realizing that I could do it. "
Christy, 20, North Carolina

What have you learned by studying abroad?

"I have learned more about the person that I am and what I am capable of. I have also learned that the world is much more complicated than most people think. It is very large place with many people, all with different priorities and influences – yet, at the core, people are the same."
Nick, 22, Ohio

"I learned independence studying abroad. I was used to being just a few hours drive from my parents at home, but when there is an ocean separating you, it's hard to get home just to take a breather. I learned how to make my own travel arrangements, how to maneuver through huge international cities and airports where I didn't speak the language, and how to identify my own comfort zones. I could feel myself stepping out of them frequently and it was definitely exciting!"
Laurel, 22, North Carolina

"There are several things I have learned while studying abroad. I have learned all about a new culture. This is great when I meet someone from England abroad, as we'll have something to talk about instantly. I also really enjoy being able to find my way around one of the world's greatest capitals without having to look at a map. It's the little things like that that makes one appreciate having studied in London, for example. I have also learned that distance is very relative – coming from a small town, I was shocked at the amount of time it took to travel into the centre of London!"
Jeroen Hoppe, 21, the Netherlands

"I learned so much by studying abroad, but one aspect that sticks out in my mind is realizing that all people are virtually the same. We may speak different languages, dress a little differently, and have different backgrounds; but, when it comes down to it, the important aspects of people are the same."
Christy, 20, North Carolina

"It is not always easy and you should be able to work out many things alone. The first time is hard to find new friends but when the first months have passed, everything becomes easier and language problems seem to disappear as well. It is important to proceed with your plans and not to give up. Everything will become normal for you, but it takes time to feel well in the new country and neighborhood.

You meet the most interesting people in your life and make many new friends. There are so many international students and you are never alone. You only have to take part in activities and it is easy to meet new people. I did not know anybody when I came to London. The first three months were awful because I was always alone. But when university started finally in September, I soon made new friends and, after a few months at university, I started to love this place. If you live on campus, it might be even easier to meet people, but I lived in Central London had no contact to students before my lectures started."
Bastian, 23, Germany

"A lot of things. It forced me to learn how to be more patient with people, appreciate people more. I have learned that all people are very different, individual, and intelligent in their own way. I would even say that studying abroad has changed my vision of life in general. I learned to respect myself and others more, to believe in my strength."
Anastasia, 20, Russia

"I learned so much more than what was taught within the four walls of the classroom. I learned to be self sufficient, a better compromiser and 'what makes people tick.' The last thing is the reason I went abroad. For fear of sounding cliché, I'll say I wanted to learn about other cultures, the history of the people and the land. It's funny now to be able to say, 'yeah, I was at Stonehenge', or 'oh yeah once when I was at the Guinness Beer Brewery...' Or to think back fondly of all the Spanish students I met and how we laughed over my poor attempts to speak their language. I learned to just go. I was fortunate

enough to have the chance to travel through a bit of Europe. Many of these trips had only start dates and end dates. The time between flights was what I made it. I did what I wanted to do and stayed in all sorts of places. That was one of the best times of my life. I will never forget the friends there."
Mary Kate, 23, Massachusetts

"Studying abroad taught me to be a very independent person. You are forced to take responsibility for yourself because no one else there is going to be able to. Learning to adjust to new customs and live in lifestyles that you may not be accustomed to are all great parts about studying in the UK."
Jeff, 20, North Carolina

"I learned a very important lesson very quickly upon arriving in London. I remember riding on the tube on one of my first days in the city and taking a look around me. Sitting to the right of me was a lady speaking French. Sitting to the left of me was a child speaking a language I didn't recognize. Standing in front of me were some people speaking British. Then there was me. There I was, an American learning just how small my place in the world was. I was just one person, one nationality among several."
Caroline, 20, North Carolina

If you could give a student who is about to leave to study in the UK advice before they leave, what would you tell them?

"I would tell them to not be afraid of challenging themselves. Great things come out of great challenges. Studying abroad is not always for everyone; but, if a person is willing to open their mind and find out what the world has to offer, it can be a beautiful place. And a place with great opportunities to learn about yourself and your neighbors on this planet."
Nick, 22, Ohio

"The UK is such a diverse place. The countryside is absolutely gorgeous and the cities are spectacular. London always has something going on, but the smaller cities have so much character of their own! It's great getting out to see all

the other countries in Europe when you can, but don't neglect the little island you're on. See as much of that as you can. It's exciting and different. You rarely see the same thing twice! Don't be afraid to look like a tourist, it's the only way you'll get to see and do all the things that will make studying abroad the most memorable experience of your life!"
Laurel, 22, North Carolina

"Expect the beginning of your study abroad experience to be difficult and allow for an adjustment period. It can be a little overwhelming in the beginning getting used to new surroundings and trying to meet people. But join all the activities you can and know that it's only a matter of time before you're having experiences that you will remember for the rest of your life."
Christy, 20, North Carolina

"Try to find a job as soon as possible to support yourself financially. Also, don't be afraid to talk to strangers, especially during the first year of your study. Remember that everyone is in the same boat as you: no-one knows anyone, and you're likely to make friends just by chatting to people randomly during the introduction night. The first weeks of university are the most fun in your life. Talk to as many people as possible and get a feel of what people are like. And, most of all, enjoy yourself!"
Jeroen, 21, the Netherlands

"They should get information about the living costs because it is not as cheap as expected. All amounts given in research are amounts, which cover the basics; traveling, etc. is not included! One should organize the financial background before leaving. A student should have good language skills because during lectures nobody speaks slowly because you are a foreigner. And, of course, you should be able- without any help- to organize your schedules, NHS care, bank account, renting a flat, etc. It is also important to organize things from home so that the majority will be prepared when you are arriving in your foreign destination.

It is always good to visit your new place of living and studying before you actually move, if it is possible. Because, for many students it looks amazing in photos or prospectus; but, when they are directly at the location, they start to hate it. Therefore, it is always important to choose the place of study very carefully. Some people prefer smaller places and some people love cities. Make up your own mind and then go for it."
Bastian, 23, Germany

"Stay calm! Don't panic at first signs of what seems to be depression or anxiety. Smile and never be afraid to ask questions or ask for help! NEVER! We are all just humans and should be capable of understanding and giving support! Remember, finding friends and settling in the new place is a lot easier than it seems!"
Anastasia, 20, Russia

"It is most important to be open for everything that waits for you. There is much more out there than you might think of or expect. But whatever it is, it will lead you a step further into the whole experience; into becoming a part of the culture you have entered and the community you and the fellow international students form. Sometimes we stumble over things, but very often we really need to hold our eyes open to notice a slight but significant difference. It is important to hear the many voices of fellow international students with their variety of experiences and backgrounds. To give in order to receive. To be a part of it. To make something happen and have influence over other people's experience makes it worthwhile for all of you. It is great to mingle with home students to get a better insight into the country you chose to study in. Yet the many evenings of endless talking and silence, of shared longing or home sickness, feelings of loss and growing up, with people in the same situation will make an even deeper impression on you and that can lead to intense friendship that lasts longer than the course."
Kathrin, 21, Germany

"One receives so much advice from people who have gone before, and from others who have never even ventured outside their own state, that 90% of it gets jumbled into a useless inaccessible mass. The best piece of advice is to have very few expectations. Do expect to have a good time, but be able to roll with the punches. Travels plans may need to be repeatedly amended. Classes and friends will change. Not much will be what you expect; other cultures have a way of not really falling into your pre-conceived stereotypes. If and when the opportunity to travel outside your curriculum presents itself, take it and pay for it (financially) later. When will you be back? So take advantage of opportunities."
Mary Kate, 23, Massachusetts

"Before leaving for the U.K., try to make contacts with the school you will be attending and any students that may be studying abroad at the same time you will be. It helps to have someone you know and be familiar with a name so you are not so lost when first arriving."
Jeff, 20, North Carolina

"The one piece of advice I could give a student preparing to travel abroad is to read, read, read. Learn about the country you are going to, the culture, the customs, traditions, etc.. Stay up to date on current events and world politics."
Caroline, 20, North Carolina

"Pack as little as you can when you leave to study abroad. I accumulated so many mementos that I ended up leaving several items I was not attached to and buying three additional suitcases to get my things home."
Caroline, 20, North Carolina

Chapter 9
Getting ready to return home

Once you have spent six months to three years collecting souvenirs, how do you get them home? Returning is probably one of the most complicated times for students. You have been abroad for some time and managed to save a lot of things; school work, papers, books, souvenirs, mementos, and gifts. You may have bought a little something for everyone you know, and you also have the extra clothes, shoes, and goodies that you have accumulated during your stay.

Packing Your Bags

Perhaps the most puzzling situation that you will find yourself in during your entire time abroad is packing to return home. Most students will have come to the UK well within their luggage allowance and then bought items like clothes and shoes while there. Add to this your entire course materials, the things you bought for your dorm room, and all the gifts and souvenirs you have collected. This will mean that most students could easily use twice the luggage allowance when they return home! There are a few tips that I can recommend to ease this situation.

The first idea is to send things home gradually when people come to visit. Ask anyone who comes to see you to take a few items *remember this* ↙

back with them. This will be a big help. If your parents or family members are coming, ask them to bring an empty suitcase that you can fill with items that you won't need for the remainder of the trip. That way you can send items home that you have never worn or that are out of season, like a winter coat. This way you will be able to send more home at no cost to you. If friends and family can help, you will find it will be easier to pack for your journey home.

Once you have sent as much material with others as possible, you have to decide what you can and cannot take with you. The luggage allowance on your return flight will be the same as the outward flight if you are on the same airline, generally two check-in bags that do not weigh over 70 pounds each, plus one carry on and one personal item. You need to call the airline and make sure that these are indeed the limits as they are subject to change and every airline is different. Ask about a size allowance too. Each bag must be within a certain size, calculated by adding together the height, width, and length of the item. Once you have the weight and size allowance for your airline, then you can start to make some decisions.

In Chapter Two I recommended that you bring some items that can be left behind at the end of your experience. For example, towels or any bedding that you have brought would be good choices. You may also need to leave items that you purchased for your dorm. Those inexpensive electronics will not work at home, but someone else can use them. See if there is a place to donate them on campus for students who will come in the future; otherwise, leave them with friends who may be remaining for another semester. You may want to take some items to the local charity shop where someone else can buy and use them, but do not take electrical items as charity shops are prohibited from selling them for safety reasons. Consider what you really need to take home, and leave everything else.

Have a trial packing session at least a week before you leave. If you wait until the last night and discover that you have too much, you may not have time to post anything or leave it for others. You will also discover if you are over the weight limit or if you have room for one last shopping spree. Pack your suitcases and weigh them so that you know where you stand.

If you are over the weight limit, you can be charged extra at the airport or be in the unfortunate situation of repacking at the airport check in. Try to go through you items several times before you depart and see what you can leave. If there is nothing that you can part with, you will have to choose between paying extra to take it home or posting it to yourself.

Posting Items Home

If you decide to post things consider paper and books first. These go at a reduced rate. Also, take advantage of surface rates rather than air mail. It will take much longer to arrive, but you will pay less. Do not pack anything in a package that will go surface if you will need it immediately. Once you have left these in the hands of the post office, it may be three months before you see them again. I have posted many packages this way between the two countries and never had a problem receiving the goods. I have had to wait some time before they arrived, but I did plan ahead and sent them well before I needed them again.

Getting to the Airport

After you have rehearsed packing your luggage to make sure that everything fits and is within the luggage weight allowance, you will need to think about how to get to the airport. If the university offers a shuttle service or any type of transfer, take this. It is almost impossible to negotiate public transportation on your own with two seventy pound bags and your carry-on items. If you must take public transportation, leave early and give yourself plenty of time. You will need the extra time to get to your destination with all of your bags. You may want to budget for a taxi or try to find a friend to share one with. Although the taxi may be quite an expense, the convenience of being picked up at your door and dropped at the airport entrance is worth it.

You will need to start thinking about this airport journey a week or so before you depart. If you have friends that are leaving at the same time, try to share a ride with them. If you need to book the university transportation, do so early to ensure a reservation. If you are taking public transport, research the route and give yourself plenty of time for mistakes, time to rest if you are carrying bags, and time to negotiate stairs and long walks with suitcases.

When taking an international flight you will need to be at the airport a minimum of two hours early. This gives you time to check in and deal with any problems should they arise. When arranging your travel, plan to get to the airport two hours before your flight. That means that you may have to leave your university three or four hours before the flight time. It is always better to be early and have an opportunity to shop, pick up last minute souvenirs, or get something to eat. As I suggested for your outbound trip, take a snack in your carry-on in case the airline food is inedible. If you do not arrive early and have problems in any way, you may be racing to catch your flight, a situation that no one looks forward to.

Other Suggestions

Your departure date may be set by the day that your accommodations contract finishes. If you are in university accommodations or in a flat off campus, you will have paid a deposit. To get this deposit returned, the landlord or university may want to see the condition of the room when you leave it. Allow some time for this and negotiate for the inspection just before you leave. You need to speak to your landlord or university about this because they may issue you a refund check in pounds which you will need to cash in the UK. If you return to the US with one of these checks, it may cost more in bank fees to cash it than it is worth.

In the two weeks before you leave, you should begin to negotiate this process. Speak to the appropriate representative and explain the need for obtaining the refund before you leave the country. Most universities and landlords will understand. If they insist on sending a check to you once you have returned home, ask and see if they can credit it to a credit card or wire the money to you. If they can only send a check, do the best you can to negotiate with your bank.

If you have opened a bank account in the UK, you will need to visit the bank to close this account. You will need to give the bank your debit card or check guarantee card and your check book. It may take the bank some time to ensure you have no outstanding debts on the account before they will close it. I would suggest going to close the account at least one week before you leave. Once you have closed the account, you can plan your budget for your final days in the UK. Remember that you will have airport transportation to pay for, costs at the airport if you want to buy food, gifts, or magazines, and last minute events that you will attend in the days leading up to your return home.

The final weeks or days at the university may be quite busy with going away parties, final meals, and farewells with those people who made your time abroad enjoyable. You will need to budget your time and money for the celebrations with friends. I have seen many students spend their last nights abroad with friends in the pub or having a nice meal, only to try and get everything arranged in the final hours. Waiting this long can be disastrous! Have your packing, posting, sorting, and donating to charity shops done in advance of your last days. This will give you the free time you need to enjoy your time with others.

Remember to thank everyone who made an impression. Even your lecturers and the university staff like to know when they have done a good job. You may want to send thank you cards when you return home or leave a small note for some of these people. Make sure to write down of the addresses that you want to take with you. There is a small address book included in Chapter Eleven, but you may want to add more addresses in Chapter Twelve. If you have any outstanding course work to hand in, need information on the course for your home institution, or will need to contact people at the university once you have returned, make sure that you have all of their contact details before you leave. If you are awaiting your grades, need a transcript, or have questions, these contact details will be vital. You may be able to find some of these online, but if there is a particular member of faculty who has been supportive or someone in administration with whom you have had good luck, take their names with you. This may save you many hours of frustration in trying to find them again.

It is Difficult to Leave

Most students that I speak to are anxious to return home. They miss friends and family and are ready to return to real life. Although there is anticipation about returning to your home country, it is still difficult to leave somewhere that you have studied and have made a part of your experience. Even if you have been ambivalent about the time abroad or unhappy with some aspects of it, you will still find it difficult to leave. Everyone goes through a sense a loss when the experience is over. Even more difficult than leaving the university will be leaving your new friends. Even people who live in the same country may not be close enough to visit often. You may go from spending every day with someone to not seeing them for some time.

The friendships that you make will always be a part of your memories of the trip. You may have to adjust to life at home again, but the sadness you will feel for leaving these friends who have been on this journey with you, can be overwhelming. Even if you keep in contact via e-mail and phone, the network that you had built will be different. These changes are a part of life, so give yourself the time to be sad. Leaving may be a rollercoaster of emotions from joy at seeing your family and friends to sadness in saying goodbye to others. You may even experience a sense of distress about getting on with life. These are all normal emotions and will take some time to sort out.

Many students feel better once they are with their friends and family and can talk about the experience.

The time that you had abroad will always be an amazing time in your life, and one that will hold special and unique memories. It is natural to feel sad about leaving new friends and your life abroad, but it was always a temporary arrangement. You need to try and think of the new possibilities ahead and face them with this experience to guide you. Remember how you felt in the first weeks abroad and when you left to start your journey? This may well be the same feelings that you have as you leave for home again.

Chapter 10
Home again

Returning home to restart your life can be a very difficult time. You may find that the place you left is different. Your friends may have graduated, moved, or formed new friendships while you were away. You will have changed as well. You may have matured or found new interests. You may also find it difficult to speak to friends and family about places they have never been to or things they have never experienced. Think of the times when you have looked at someone's vacation photos or heard their travel stories. Others may feel this way when you are relating your experience to them. It is never the same as having been there.

The friends and college mates that you left behind to study abroad may be jealous of the fact that you were able to go. They may also simply not understand your experiences and it may be difficult to talk with them. Many students find that they return home and it seems as though they never left. When they do talk about their experiences abroad, it seems like a dream or something that never really happened. It may seem especially so when you are spending time with those who were not there and can't participate in stories and reminiscing.

Reentering life at home can be as much of a shock as when you left. Give yourself time to grieve for the experience that has passed. Don't linger too long with this, but work out constructive ways to become re-involved. Be patient with friends and family. Once you have caught back up to life at home you will have more common ground. Turn the experience you had abroad into a positive for others, perhaps for new foreign students or communities, which you are now more able to help.

The culture shock that you experienced when you first moved abroad will now be replaced by reverse culture shock and will need the same readjustment as when you moved. At first it may have been strange to walk everywhere when in your first weeks in the UK, but now it may be odd to go everywhere in a car. These aspects of reverse culture shock are unnerving because we don't expect it. If you lived in a culture once, then it should be easy to live in it again. But research has even shown that this process moves in cycles where you may have difficulties adjusting one week, yet feel at home the next. This cycle will continue from week to week. Don't underestimate how hard it can be to re-acculturate yourself, and remember that everyone goes through this process.

The most difficult thing to adjust to may be the changes in yourself. In your time abroad you may have become much more independent and self sufficient. After months abroad of negotiating with the university, your living environment, and a new city, you will find that you have a new confidence about taking care of yourself. This confidence may be new to your family and friends. It will take them some time to adjust and to understand all of these changes.

You may want to alter the relationships with those around you when you return, and this will be difficult for those involved to understand. If you had always been dependent on your parents, family, boyfriend or girlfriend, but have found self sufficiency while abroad, they may have difficulty understanding this. Although this is a natural part of growing up, the experience may be more startling when it comes to study abroad. You may have packed a lot of growing and maturing into a small period of time. The strength that you have gained from dealing with difficult times abroad may have made you a different person in some ways, so let others adjust gradually to the new you. It may be a difficult transition but a necessary one.

You may experience a change in your opinion of your home country. You may have spent months speaking to others from around the world about how your country is viewed. These conversations, as well as seeing life lived a different way and what you have learned academically, may alter your view of where you live. You may start to see your world as smaller or how your culture is one of many. This change in world view may seem odd to those around you who have not had your experience.

Give yourself time to adjust to changes in the environment, changes in culture, changes in family and friends, and changes in yourself. Reverse culture shock when you return home is like starting over. It may take weeks or months to readjust to life at home. Everyone goes through this and rest assured that you are not alone. If you can keep in touch with friends you made while abroad who are also returning, you may be able to create a network to share your frustrations. Also, explaining your feelings to friends and family will help them understand the difficulties you may be having. Take time to readjust and try the ideas for sharing your experience listed below. They may help with this part of the journey.

Ideas for Sharing Your Experience with Others

Memories
- Make a scrapbook

- Write your own story about living abroad

- Write and perform a comedy sketch about some of the stranger things that happened along the way

- Have your video tapes edited into a movie about your time abroad

- Create a web page for all of your friends and family to see your trip

- Submit an article to your university newspaper about your experience

- Write an article for your local newspaper about a location that you visited

- Make a collage of information from all of the places you have visited

- Keep e-mailing those friends you made while abroad

- Arrange a reunion of the people you miss the most

- Write down all of the names of people you knew while abroad and put them with their photos. You will be amazed at how quickly you will forget otherwise

- Make a top ten list of the places that you visited in your host country

- Make a top ten list of places and events that happened while traveling abroad

- Make a bottom ten list of your experience abroad!

- Cook a dinner for your friends and family that is typical of what you ate while abroad. You may have to look for the groceries, but it is a great way to share some of your experience

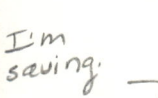

- Retrieve all the e-mails you sent friends and family and use these to remember what you did and how you felt

- Draw a map of the area you lived in and identify all of the shops, transportation links, and favorite places

- Plan an itinerary for a vacation that you would take with a friend to visit where you lived. Make plans for each day for what you would want to show them, where you would eat, and the transportation links between places

Volunteering and Meeting Others
- Volunteer for your university's study abroad office

- Make friends with an international student once you have returned home

- Volunteer for groups that support international missions or community groups that emphasize different cultures

- Join a cultural group in your home city that supports the culture of the country you have studied in

- Continue to read travel books and books about your host country. Nothing will make you feel there as much as a good bookshop and a warm cup of coffee

- Start a study abroad alumni group at your university

- Have coffee mornings with students who have studied abroad. It is a great way to speak to people who understand your stories

- Have an international fair at your university or college. Invite people to cook foods from different countries and share their traditions

- Study a new language. This is a great way to make friends who have traveled abroad or have an interest in different cultures

- Write a guide for students who are going to your university and tell them all the details that you wish you would have known

- Fly the British flag. You will be amazed how many people from the UK are in your area

- Volunteer to speak with other students about study abroad opportunities

Helping Yourself Cope

- Find a restaurant that reminds you of your time abroad and promise to eat there when you get "homesick"

- Send letters to all of your friends from abroad and tell them how much you miss them

- Send letters to your friends and family at home to tell them how much their support meant to you

- Make a list of all of the things that you missed from your home country while abroad and think about how happy you are to have them back

- Read the newspaper from abroad on-line

- Find a store that sells food from your host country, there is nothing like English chocolate to help ease the pain of separation

- Watch for low, off season airfares so you can return for a visit

- Write your resume to reflect the international experience you now have

- Keep a journal of the time when you return and are going through reverse culture shock

- Try to write down all of the ways that you have changed. This will help you see the positive ways that you have grown

- Allow yourself to be sad when you feel like it, but don't be sad for too long. Try to counter this with all of the fun memories that you have

- Write a list of ten adjectives that described you before you left and ten that describe you upon your return

Using the list above may help you to put your trip into perspective. If you can make the most of your memories, help others by volunteering, and find ways to cope with the times when you are sad or miss study abroad, you will have an easier time through this period. Remember that new adventures in life require adjustment and change. By using strategies to cope with the ups and downs of new situations, you will identify tools to handle potentially difficult times.

Chapter 11
My Trip

Here is an opportunity for you to make your own trip notes and journal. The worksheets follow each chapter in the book, and you may want to work on some of the early chapters even before you have left on your trip. These pages are designed to provide an order to your planning and a place to keep organized. The side benefit is that they may well be memories that you will keep for years to come. Have fun with this chapter, and use it to personalize your journey and your information.

We begin with pre-departure basics followed by the first two weeks. These journal entries will be the basic facts and details that you will need, including budget examples and class information sheets. The other entries from living abroad and traveling are more personal and can be guides to help you think about what you like, what you dislike, and your hopes for traveling while abroad. The final sheets will prepare you to return home and give you an opportunity for some valuable reflection on your experience in retrospect.

Pre Departure:

My new university:
_____
_____

Arrival Date:
_____
_____

Date classes start:
_____
_____

Flight Information:
_____
_____

Name of my international officer and contact details:
_____
_____

Accommodation name and address:
_____
_____
_____
_____

Classes I am registered/ registering for, dates, times, and professors:
_____
_____
_____
_____
_____
_____

My Trip 113

Phone numbers for the university:

_____
_____

Emergency contact number in the US:

_____
_____

Flight date, time and number:

_____
_____

Arrival information (who to meet and where):

_____
_____

Travel information if not being met:

_____
_____
_____
_____

Other:

_____
_____
_____
_____
_____
_____
_____

First Week

Information that you will need to know, information about your new accommodation and the activities at the university.

My new address and phone number:
_____
_____
_____

My new flat mates:
_____
_____
_____
_____
_____
_____
_____

Closest grocery store and its opening hours:
_____
_____
_____

Bank account details:
_____
_____
_____
_____

Health Service information:
_____
_____
_____
_____

International and student group trips and information:

_____
_____
_____
_____
_____

Other campus groups that I want to be involved with:

_____
_____
_____
_____
_____

Orientation date, location and time:

_____
_____

Registration date and time:

_____
_____

Schedule to meet professors and international office:

_____
_____
_____
_____
_____

Problems and concerns:

_____
_____
_____

Who to talk to about these problems and concerns:

_____
_____
_____
_____
_____
_____

Other Important Issues:

_____
_____
_____
_____

Budget

This is a sample budget as discussed in chapter 2. Try and use it as a guide to personalize one for yourself.

	Rent	**Bills**	**Food**	**Entertainment**	**Extra Expenses**	**Total**
Date						
Week 1	£	£	£	£	£	£
Week 2	£	£	£	£	£	£
Week 3	£	£	£	£	£	£

Travel Budget

	Airfare	Hotel/ Hostel	Food	Sightseeing	Other Transportation	Total
Place		*Per night*			*To and from the airport/while visiting*	
Place 1	£	£	£	£	£	£
Place 2	£	£	£	£	£	£
Place 3	£	£	£	£	£	£

Academics

Information about the courses for which I am registered, times and dates that they meet, and assessments for each class.

Class 1:
    Course Title: _____
    Professor: _____
    Classroom: _____
    Times and dates: _____
    Any cancelled classes: _____
    Books needed: _____
    _____
    _____
    Assessment type: _____
    Assessment Due Date or exam date: _____

Class 2:
    Course Title: _____
    Professor: _____
    Classroom: _____
    Times and dates: _____
    Any cancelled classes: _____
    Books needed: _____
    _____
    _____
    Assessment type: _____
    Assessment Due Date or exam date: _____

Class 3:
    Course Title: _____
    Professor: _____
    Classroom: _____
    Times and dates: _____
    Any cancelled classes: _____
    Books needed: _____
    _____
    Assessment type: _____
    Assessment Due Date or exam date: _____

Class 4:
    Course Title: _____
    Professor: _____
    Classroom: _____
    Times and dates: _____
    Books needed: _____
    _____

    Any cancelled classes: _____
    Assessment type: _____
    Assessment Due Date or exam date: _____

Class 5:
    Course Title: _____
    Professor: _____
    Classroom: _____
    Times and dates: _____
    Any cancelled classes: _____
    Books needed: _____
    _____

    Assessment type: _____
    Assessment Due Date or exam date: _____

Plans for these assessments:
_____
_____
_____

Concerns about the courses you are taking:
_____
_____
_____
_____

Living in the UK

My favorite part of studying abroad:

My least favorite part of studying abroad:

The most frustrating thing about this experience:

The best thing about this experience:

My favorite places on campus:

My favorite places off campus:

My favorite restaurant:

My favorite pub / club / student hang out:

My favorite class:

The best thing to do on the weekend:

Additional Information:

Appendix A:
My Journal

My Journal

Appendix B: Useful Web Addresses

Airline Websites

Air Canada	www.aircanada.ca
American Airlines	www.aa.com
Continental Airlines	www.continental.com
Delta Airlines	www.delta.com
KLM	www.klm.com
Northwest	www.nwa.com
United Airlines	www.ual.com
US Airways	www.usairways.com
Virgin Airlines	www.virgin.com

Other Travel Sites

Travel Advisories	http://travel.state.gov/travel_warnings.html

UK Weather	www.weather.com
UK News	www.bbc.co.uk

Groceries in the UK

Safeway	www.safeway.co.uk
Sainsburys	www.sainsburys.co.uk
Tesco	www.tesco.com
Waitrose	www.waitrose.com

Travel in the UK websites

Trains

www.trainline.com

www.rail.co.uk

www.virgin.com

Tube

www.londontransport.co.uk

Buses

www.londontransport.co.uk

Holidays in the UK

www.stagecoach.co.uk

Places to visit

English Heritage	www.englishheritage.org.uk
National Trust	www.nationaltrust.org.uk

City and Places of Interest Website

Bath	www.visitbath.co.uk
Belfast	www.discovernorthernireland.com

Birmingham	www.birmingham.org.uk
Bournemouth	www.bournemouth.co.uk
Brighton	www.brighton.co.uk
Cambridge	www.cambridge.gov.uk
Cardiff	www.cardiff.gov.uk
Corfe Castle	www.corfecastle.org.uk
The Cotswold's	www.cotswolds-calling.com
Dover	www.whitecliffscountry.org.uk
Dover Castle	www.tourist-information-uk.com/dover-castle.htm
Durham	www.durham.gov.uk
Edinburgh	www.edinburgh.org
Glasgow	www.glasgowguide.co.uk
Hadrian's Wall	www.hadrians-wall.org
Inverness	www.inverness-scotland.com
Isle of Skye	www.skye.co.uk
The Lake District	www.lake-district.gov.uk
Leeds	www.leeds.gov.uk
Leeds Castle	www.leeds-castle.co.uk
Liverpool	www.visitliverpool.com

Loch Ness	www.lochness.co.uk
London	www.londontouristboard.co.uk
Manchester	www.manchester.gov.uk/visitorcentre
Newcastle	www.newcastle.gov.uk
Oxford	www.oxfordcity.co.uk
Saint Andrews	www.saint-andrews.co.uk
Salisbury	www.visitsalisburyuk.com
Snowdonia	www.wales-tourist-information.co.uk
Sterling Castle	www.historic-scotland.gov.uk
Stonehenge	www.english-heritage.org.uk
Stratford upon Avon	www.shakespeare-country.co.uk
Warwick Castle	www.warwick-castle.co.uk
Winchester	www.winchester.gov.uk
Windsor Castle	www.royal.gov.uk
York	www.york-tourism.co.uk

Travel outside of the UK websites

Budget Airlines

Easyjet	www.easyjet.co.uk
Ryan Air	www.ryanair.co.uk
BMI	www.flybmi.com

Useful Web Addresses

Eurostar	www.eurostar.com
Eurail	www.eurail.com

Ferry companies

Sea France	www.seafrance.co.uk
Hover Speed	www.hoverspeed.com
Brittany Ferries	www.brittany-ferries.com
Stena Line	www.stenaline.com

Youth Hostels

www.yha.co.uk

www.hostels.com

General Travel Sites

Expedia	www.expedia.co.uk
STA	www.sta.com
Last Minute	www.lastminute.com
Contiki Tours	www.contiki.com

Other useful pages

British Council	www.britishcouncil.org
British Consulate	www.britianusa.com
Home Office	www.homeoffice.gov.uk

Author

Dr. Holly Carter holds a Ph.D. in Sociology and Health Services Research from the University of North Texas. In addition she has a Masters degree in public health from the University of North Texas Health Science Centre in Fort Worth, Texas, a Masters in Philosophy in Sociology from the University of Glasgow in Glasgow, Scotland, and a Masters of Science in Social Work from the University of Texas at Arlington. Her undergraduate degree is from Midwestern State University in Texas. She has a graduate certificate in Teaching and Learning in Higher Education from Roehampton University of Surrey in London.

Currently Dr. Carter is an assistant professor in the Department of Sociology at Augusta State University in Augusta, Georgia. Her academic interests include international education and comparative health care delivery systems. Her hobbies are travel and her two dogs, Rugby and Windsor.

Index

A

A & E, 47
A to Z guides, 47
academic pitfalls, 39
academics, 118
accommodation, 6, 21, 112
adaptor, 9
air travel, 14
airfare, 71
airport, 99
alarm clock, 12
arrival date, 112
arrival information, 113
ASDA, 46
assessment, 34

B

bank, 41
bank account, 42, 100, 114
bank statement, 8
Bath, 63
Belfast, 68
Belgium- Brussels, Bruges, 76
bills, 42
Birmingham, 63
BMI Baby, 72
Bournemouth, 63
Brighton, 63
British consulate, 8, 13
Britrail Pass, 69
budget, 25, 116
budget carriers, 72
buses, 60
business hours, 50
buying clothes, 47
buying shoes, 48

C

calling cards, 48
Cambridge, 63
Cardiff, 69
catered, 21
cell phones, 48
classes, 33, 112
converter, 9
Co-Op, 46
Corfe Castle/ The Dorset Coast, 66
Cotswold's, 64

course convener, 32
course information, 16
credit/ debit cards, 48
customs, 20

D

day pass, 61
Delta card, 43
deposit, 100
doctor, 41
Dover Castle, 66
driver's permit, 41
Durham, 64

E

Easter break, 39
EasyJet, 72
eating at restaurants, 49
eating in a pub, 49
Edinburgh, 67
electronic devices, 9
emergency calls, 49
emotions, 28
essay, 33, 34, 35
Eurail Pass, 69, 73
Eurostar, 71, 74
exams, 37
external marker, 38

F

final exam, 33
flight, 113
floors, 50
foreign exchange, 42
France- Paris, 75
free refills, 49
fresher's week, 23, 24
frustration, 28

G

gas/ petrol, 50
Glasgow, 68
grades, 38
groceries, 50
grocery shopping, 46

H

Hadrian's Wall, 67
head of school, 32
health service, 114
Hershey's bars, 46
Home Office, 14, 27
Hostels, 74
household/ dorm room items, 9

I

immigration, 6, 19
immigration information, 16
international center, 23
international officer, 112
Inverness/ Loch Ness, 68
invigilating, 37
Ireland - Dublin, 78
ISIC international student identity card, 25
Isle of Skye, 68
Italy - Rome, Pisa, Venice, 77

J

jet lag, 22
jobs, 27

L

Lake District, the, 64
laptop computer, 9
lecture, 34
Leeds, 64
Leeds Castle, 67

Liverpool, 64
living expense budget, 26
local calls, 50
London, 64
luggage allowance, 12

M

Manchester, 65
medications, 11
medicines, 43
meet and greet service, 20
memories, 105

N

National Health Service, 43
national insurance card, 28
Netherlands- Amsterdam, 77
Network Rail, 60
Newcastle, 65

O

off license, 51
orientation, 6, 7, 23, 115
Oxford, 65

P

packing, 8, 12, 97
packing guide, 17
passport control, 8, 13
pay phones, 51
paying on buses, 51
photographs, 12
post office, 41
postage stamps, 42
posting items home, 99
practical information, 16
pre departure information, 6, 112
prescription, 11, 44
professors, 23, 33
program information, 7

prospectus, 6
public transportation, 14, 59
pubs, 21, 45

Q

queuing, 54

R

rector, 32
register for classes, 23
registering with police, 24
registering your passport, 24
registration, 115
registry, 32
restaurants, 44
Ryanair, 72

S

Safeway, 46
Sainsbury's, 46
sales tax, 51
Salisbury/ Stonehenge, 65
schedule, 115
second marking, 38
shipping, 13
shopping, 52
Snowdonia National Park, 69
Sommerfield, 46
Spain – Madrid and Ibiza, 77
St Andrews, 68
Sterling/ Sterling Castle, 68
store opening hours, 52
Stratford Upon Avon, 65
student identification cards, 24
subway, 61
Switch card, 43

T

taxis, 20, 52, 61
television, 53

Tesco's, 46
time, 53
timetables, 39
tipping, 53
titles, 33
train tickets, 53
trains, 60
travel budget, 26, 117
travel cost worksheet, 79
travel guide, 62
travel information, 113
TV license, 41, 42

U

umbrella, 11

V

VAT, 13

visas, 8, 13
volunteering, 106

W

Waitrose, 46
Warwick Castle, 67
washing facilities, 10
water, 54
weekend pass, 61
Winchester, 66
Windsor Castle, 67

Y

York, 66
Young Person's Railcard, 60
youth cards, 25